Marcelo Sena

The Archdiocese

Marcelo Sena

The Archdiocese

Communism and Catholic Reform in the plot of the 1960s

ScienciaScripts

Imprint

Cover image: www.ingimage.com

This book is a translation from the original published under ISBN 978-3-330-76185-8.

Publisher:
Sciencia Scripts
is a trademark of
Dodo Books Indian Ocean Ltd. and OmniScriptum S.R.L publishing group

120 High Road, East Finchley, London, N2 9ED, United Kingdom
Str. Armeneasca 28/1, office 1, Chisinau MD-2012, Republic of Moldova, Europe
Managing Directors: Ieva Konstantinova, Victoria Ursu
info@omniscriptum.com

Printed at: see last page
ISBN: 978-620-8-37957-5

SUMMARY

Presentation

This research consists of a Communication Content Analysis of texts (or recording units) published in the newspaper O Arquidiocesano during its first eight years of publication. To this end, categories of analysis were defined, based on specific criteria for coding the data related to the publications.

The hypothesis of this analysis is to prove the political participation of the Catholic Church at its grassroots level, also from the official media, in the period mentioned above, which consists of the years 1959 to 1967. In addition to proving this, the aim is to understand how the institution approaches the process of internal transformations it experienced during this period.

The aim was to identify the mechanisms used by the newspaper to disseminate the ideologies of the Catholic Church, by perceiving O Arquidiocesano as the "Official Organ of the Archdiocese of Mariana". As a priority, we looked at the frequency with which the content appeared, related to the specificities of each insertion context.

In order to do this, it was necessary to investigate the historical context in which the issues were cut. Therefore, chapter 1 of this work corresponds to historical contextualisation, which influences the process of disseminating content and statements.

The second chapter refers to coding and processing the data according to pre-established categories. This process is responsible for generating the incidence indices, which can be related to each other and to the historical variables and, consequently, make it possible to interpret and identify the implicit characteristics of this communication situation. In this chapter, it is also possible to understand some peculiarities of the messages and statements published.

The third chapter consists of interpreting the indices and therefore explaining the results obtained from the coding process. This chapter is based on a qualitative approach to the coded data. The data provides inferences about the conditions under which the messages were produced.

This work also provides a possible index for cataloguing The Archdiocesan, facilitating the emergence of other research related to this communication process.

CHAPTER 1

The weather

The 1960s saw transformations in the political and social structure of the main economic powers of the time, as Jurgen Habermas suggests in "Structural Change in the Public Sphere"[1] . The environment created by the Cold War, following the Second World War in 1945, in this period caused a polarisation between the communist and capitalist ideologies represented, respectively, by the Soviet Union and the United States.

Influenced by them, some organisations under siege in Brazil also took a stance on world events involving the ideologies in question. What's more, as the bipolarity between the ideologies grew, so did the pressure for government representatives to take sides.

Institutions with international reach, such as the Catholic Church, also underwent changes and were urged to reiterate or ratify discourses related to the political instability arising from the ideological clash between communists and capitalists. At the same time, the leadership of the Church was concerned with maintaining the traditional Catholic hierarchical structure. In this way, the Church seeks to adapt to the needs of modern society without, however, diminishing its control over Catholic offices.

The Church distinguished itself from other institutions of the time by structuring its hegemony on religious discourse. For Pierre Bourdieu, *"(...) religion is predisposed to assume an ideological function, a practical and political function of absolutising the relative and legitimising the arbitrary. "* (BOURDIEU apud PAMPLONA, 2008, p. 8). Thus, religious discourse is self-affirming in itself and, in theory, does not need other mechanisms to prove its veracity.

> "By justifying the hegemony of the dominant classes and symbolically reinforcing the resignation of the dominated party, the institution not only guarantees the reproduction of the *status*

[1] See Habermas, 1984.

quo, but also its own survival ."[2]

Based on the assumption that religious discourse is sacralised (or shielded), the Church tends to justify existing social structures and contribute to maintaining the dominant classes as holders of political and economic power. In this way, revolutionary ideologies that challenged the social reality of the working classes and based their discourse on breaking with the prevailing order were seen as a threat to the Church, an institution with an ancient hierarchy, in certain contexts linked to conservative elites.

1.1 The Catholic Church

In order to understand the political participation of the Catholic Church in the period covered by the analytical corpus, an attempt was made to identify, albeit superficially, aspects of Catholic action in the historical context of the 20th century that may have influenced the construction of the discourses in force during the 1960s.

At the beginning of the 20th century, Catholic doctrine developed on the basis of the concept of the "new Christendom". While colonial Christendom was based on relations between the Catholic Church and the dominant oligarchies, the new Christendom accompanied the development of capitalism and liberalism until the mid-1910s. From the capitalist crisis, which began in 1930, there was an evolution in Catholic thought, bringing it closer to the popular sectors and the middle classes, especially in Latin America. Pablo Richards (1979, p. 99) emphasises the Church's relationship with the state and civil society during this period:

> "We therefore believe that the new Christendom, as an inadequate response to the crisis of colonial Christendom, has undoubtedly emphasised the antagonistic contradiction between *Christendom* and *the Church* throughout the 1808-1960 cycle. We have seen throughout our previous historical analysis that the basic structure of Christendom - always maintained and never criticised - consists of the dual relationship of Church-State and Church-Society. The Church seeks to expand its influence and power in *society,* using the *State* as a mediator. The Church's relationship with civil society passes through the Church's relationship with

[2] See Pamplona, 2008, p. 8.

> society politics. Christianity, therefore, necessarily implies the Church's alliance with the system and the ruling classes."

The new Latin American Christianity, however, contributed to its own downfall from 1930 onwards, according to Richards. For the author, the concern with social injustices that Catholic thought was directed towards also served as the basis for the process of building the "Catholic Social Doctrine", which was superimposed on Christendom from the 1950s onwards.

> "If we compare the period 1870-1930 with 1930-1960, we can certainly see a remarkable evolution of the new Latin American Christianity. It has significantly broadened its social base: from a *Christianity closed* in on the narrow circle of oligarchic elites, it has evolved into a *Christianity open to* the middle classes and popular sectors. From a Church on the defensive in the fight against liberalism to a Church on the offensive in the fight against underdevelopment. From a Church that was Romanised, foreign, centralised on formal devotions and mass religious manifestations, and absorbed by family and educational problems, it moved towards a Church that was open to Latin American and national problems, concerned with the integral formation of its militants, and oriented towards social and political problems. The new Christianity evolved from conservatism to reformist and developmental social Christianity."[3]

The crisis of the capitalist system began in the 1910s. Richards (1979, p. 81) points to the First World War, in 1914, as the start of an event that had its symbolic milestone in 1929 and in which, inevitably, the social inequalities and instability of the capitalist system became evident. In addition, new governmental possibilities emerged that symbolised traces of rupture in the current social order.

> "In 1930 we have the great crisis of international monopoly capitalism and, as a consequence, in Latin America, the crisis of the Creole oligarchies and the liberal state. From 1930 onwards, the process of industrialisation spreads throughout most of the continent, and nationalist and populist movements and ideologies emerge."

[3] See Pablo Richards, 1979, p. 112

However, Richards himself emphasises that 1930 cannot be considered an absolute milestone for the crisis. The period to be understood must begin in 1914 with the start of the First World War - and end at the end of the Second World War in 1945. He evaluates the process of capitalist expansion between 1880 and 1914:

> "The articulation of the Latin American economy in dependence on international monopoly capitalism irreversibly orientates Latin America towards underdevelopment at this time. The centres of monopoly capitalism impose a development of Latin America's economic and social structure based on the export of raw materials and agricultural products, and the import of ready-made industrialised products. The link between the new colonial dependence and the domination of the liberal oligarchy, which is at the root of the growing underdevelopment of the dominated majorities, places the struggle against underdevelopment from this period onwards as a struggle against the oligarchies and national dependence. The struggle against underdevelopment and for the liberation of the masses is both an anti-oligarchic struggle and a nationalist anti-imperialist struggle. In this context, the Latin American labour movement will also develop at this time. The reconstruction of the Church, its internal reform and its redefinition within civil society also acquire new and specific characteristics during this period."[4]

As a result of the capitalist crisis in the first half of the 20th century, other possibilities arose in the face of capitalism's social injustices, including national forms of government. The Bolshevik Revolution of 1917, for example, symbolised a socialist alternative to the crisis of the capitalist system.

> "The historical novelty of the 1914-1945 crisis lies in the fact that from then on the bourgeoisie and imperialism no longer had the only solution to the crisis of capitalism, since a socialist solution to the crisis appeared for the first time with the Bolshevik Revolution of October 1917. In 1948 the People's Republic of China was formed, between 1945-1949 the bloc of socialist countries was formed, between 1950-1953 imperialism was liquidated in Korea, in 1959 the Cuban Revolution triumphed, in 1962 the People's Democratic Republic was proclaimed in Algeria, etc. At the end of the First World War, the Third Socialist International was formed, which believed that the Russian

[4] Pablo Richards, 1979, p. 80-81.

> revolution would spread throughout the world and that the International would be at the head of this revolution."[5]

The transformations experienced by the Catholic Church between the 1930s and

In the 1960s, according to Paul Richards, they were based on the conflict between the two types of Christianity: "conservative" and "populist-nationalist-Latin Americanist, culturalist and developmentalist (anti-socialist)". Richards (1979, p. 112) emphasises, however, that the Church's social approach is allied to the state and the ruling classes.

> "This new social and political insertion of the new Latin American Christianity and this considerable expansion of its social base are undoubtedly realised through the Church's alliance with the dominant classes and the state. There is thus an "ecclesiastical populism" that allows the Church to win over broad sectors of the "middle classes" and popular classes, *without breaking its alliance with the dominant classes."*

As the middle and working classes began to revolt against the system and the hegemony of the ruling classes, combined with the collapse of populist systems and the rise of popular movements, tensions arose between the discursive lines adopted by the Church to embrace the working classes and get closer to the ruling classes.

> "The situation undoubtedly changes and tends to become conflictual when these middle and popular sectors begin to act socially and politically against the system and the ruling classes. Since the Cuban Revolution of 1959, and throughout the 1960s and 1970s, Latin America has seen a growing reactivation of the popular movement, following the crisis of the capitalist system and in relation to it, and more especially with the exhaustion of the populist, nationalist and developmentalist models. The process of reactivation of the popular movement is not homogeneous and continuous throughout Latin America, but in its geographical and historical globality, it is becoming a movement in a phase of increasing expansion and deepening".[6]

From the 1950s onwards, the strands that sought to bring the Church closer

[5] Idem. P. 93.

[6] Pablo Richards, 1979, p. 113.

to the social classes grew stronger. "The decade between 1955 and 1965 saw significant changes in the Roman Catholic Church, both internationally and in Brazil. The cautious and conservative Pius XII died in 1958, and his replacement John XXIII promoted important reforms" (MAINWARING apud PAMPLONA, 2008, p. 9). Luiz Gonzaga de Souza Lima (1989, p. 30) also recognises greater social concern on the part of some sectors of the Catholic Church, both in Brazil and abroad, from the 1950s and 1960s onwards.

> "At the end of the 1950s and the beginning of the 1960s, some sectors of the Church and part of the organised Catholic world began to move closer to the movement of the dominated classes (workers, sub-proletarians) and the social forces that were fighting for changes in the social structures favourable to them."

It is important to emphasise that in an institution the size of the Church, different and even divergent positions can be perceived. Mainwaring identifies, specifically in this period, three lines of thought that overlapped in Brazilian Catholicism: the "traditionalists", the "modemising conservatives" and the "reformists".

While the traditionalists defended the maintenance of the new Christianity, the modemising conservatives believed in changing Catholicism to meet the needs of the contemporary world, basing their questions on the advance of Protestantism and communism. Reformists, on the other hand, believed "in social change as an end in itself". Lucília Delgado (2003, p. 98) also states that in institutions such as the Catholic Church, certain strands and lines of thought can be adopted.

> "In fact, the proposals and new forms proclaimed are not for the whole Church. They are specific to some more advanced sectors of groups of lay people, priests and bishops who were looking for other steps, favouring a greater dialogue with history, seeking greater participation by its members, with a view to building what they understood to be a free, just, supportive and fraternal community. The Catholic Church is not a homogenous bloc. It includes different and even contradictory practices. There are different religious and political behaviours, influenced by the

way its members are linked to the various social classes."[7]

Also in the 1950s, the National Conference of Bishops of Brazil was created. Brazil. The CNBB positioned itself, especially throughout the 1960s, as a defender of the Church's concern for social injustice. Lima (1989, p. 31) points out, however, that even this rapprochement may have been fuelled by other interests that were vital to maintaining the Catholic hierarchy in Latin America.

> "Many scholars, almost all of them foreign, unfortunately see the main cause of these bishops' actions as the desire to respond to the political threats of communism and at the same time find a new model of influence that would allow the Church to continue reaching out to the whole of society."

The Archdiocese of São Paulo, in "Brasil: nunca mais" (1985, p. 147), also explains the distance that still existed between the institutional structures of the Catholic Church and social mobilisations. The book recognises the Church's participation in the ideology created at the time, which was fundamental to the outbreak of the military coup in April 1964.

> "The overthrow of João Goulart, however, still took place at a time when the ecclesiastical areas were already sensitive to popular mobilisations. In fact, historians agree that the Church hierarchy played a fundamental role in creating an ideological climate favourable to military intervention, engaging in the anti-communist campaign sustained by the conservative elites: against Agrarian Reform, against strike movements, against the demands of the sergeants, corporals and soldiers of the Armed Forces , against the alliance of Christians and Marxists that was beginning to take place in trade unions and student bodies. "[8]

Faced with the threat posed by communism and the discursive tension that existed when approaching the social injustices caused by capitalism, the Church then developed the "Social Doctrine of the Church". *Rerum Novarum* is considered by Camacho to be the "first social encyclical of Pope Leo XIII". Published on 15 May

[7] See Ferreira, 2003, p. 98.
[8] See Archdiocese of São Paulo, 1985, p. 147.

1891, Camacho (1997, p. 50) classifies it as the "first official text of the Church that addresses the problems arising from industrial society in a global manner".

As Camacho (1995, p. 57) suggests, the encyclical can be divided into four parts: introduction - in which it recognises the situation of misery of the European working class and demands an intervention by the Church; first part - which addresses and rejects a "socialist solution"; second part - which consists of a "true solution", based on the joint action of the Church, the State and owners and workers. Although the encyclical also positions itself against liberalism, criticising it and, in a way, holding it responsible for the current social order, Camacho (1995, p. 57) concludes that "the explicit adversary of *Rerum Novarum* is socialism".

With the context of the emergence of the Church's Social Doctrine in mind, and returning to the period that makes up the analytical corpus of this work, while Pius XII had caused the Church to distance itself from the discussions of the modern world, based on the needs of the working classes, especially in the last years of his mandate (1950s), Pope John XXIII, inaugurated in 1959, summoned the Church to the Second Vatican Council. The aim of the Council was to regulate the already imminent structural reforms that the institution was experiencing in the social sphere, without losing control of the institution.

A predecessor to the Council, the encyclical *Mater Et Magistra* was published in 1961, on the occasion of the seventieth anniversary of Leo XIII's encyclical *Rerum Novarum*, and adopts the character of an update of the former.

> "[...] four parts make up the general structure of the encyclical: the first recalls the 70th anniversary of *Rerum Novarum* and gives a short summary of the social doctrine of previous pontiffs; the second offers a doctrinal synthesis that clarifies, adapts and develops previous teaching; the third addresses new aspects of the social question; the fourth and final part has a marked pastoral accent and centres on the role the Church can play in the face of these problems."[9]

The third part, among those highlighted above by Camacho, addresses

[9] See Camacho, 1995, p. 68

inequalities as the main aspect of recent social issues. Firstly, the document addresses inequalities related to development within industrialised countries, which at the same time marginalises other internal sectors, especially agriculture, and/or which affect "entire regions". However, there is greater concern about inequalities with a global impact, of which Camacho (1995, p. 76) cites the imbalance between population and means of subsistence and the "rarefaction of political relations between nations".

> "Therefore, we consider it necessary to publish this encyclical of ours, not only for a just commemoration of *Rerum Novarum*, but also so that, in accordance with the changes of the time, we may highlight and clarify in greater detail, on the one hand, the teachings of our predecessors and, on the other, clearly set out the Church's thinking on the new and most important problems of the moment."

Published just two years after Mater Et Magistra and just a few weeks before John XXIII's death, the Encyclical *Pacem in Terris* acts as a conclusion to the previous one, addressing the political issue and reflecting the Church's interest in continuing the work of the ailing pope, focusing his speech in defence of "world peace" to this end.The Cuban Revolution in 1959 contributed to the intensification of discourse from both right-wing sectors and left-wing movements about the possibilities of communist and socialist revolts in other Latin American countries. Brazil's conservative elites, represented by the agrarian or bourgeois oligarchies allied to religious power, used the fear of communist and socialist intervention in Brazil to maintain the current social order.

1.2 The Church in Mariana

Thomas Bruneau (1979, p. 21) characterises the discovery and formation of the

Colonial Brazil as "a joint venture between the Portuguese Crown and the Catholic Church, both reinforcing and legitimising each other". This alliance would have lasted until the end of the monarchical regime in 1889, and the two institutions used both mechanisms to reaffirm their existing hegemony.

"The environment was one of exploration and mission, and the tasks were to raise money for the Crown and souls for the Church. The whole of society had to be embraced: the colonisers had to be Catholic; the Indians were baptised by the missionaries and, later, the black slaves were baptised before landing in the colony. Although the Church maintained some institutions of its own, such as churches and schools, these were largely supported by the Crown, using the tithe and, in general, it was the structure of the Crown and the Church that guaranteed religion: the King was Catholic, so all his subjects were too."[10]

Also according to Bruneau (1979, p. 28), the first break between Church and State in Brazil came about with the beginning of the republican system. The Constitution promulgated on 24 February 1891[11] reduced the Church's public powers, forcing it to return to the line of structural development adopted by the Vatican.

"With the end of the Monarchy in 1889, the Church was separated from the State for the first time and removed from the public sphere, to develop separately and together with Rome. This separation and the subsequent Constitution of 1891 were abrupt and complete: freedom of worship was recognised; only civil marriages were valid; education was secularised, religion was excluded from the curriculum, and the government was prohibited from subsidising religious education; the Catholic clergy would only be supported by the state for one more year; members of religious orders engaged by the vow of obedience lost their civil rights, and so on."

After the Proclamation of the Republic and, therefore, the removal of the Church

Catholic of the emerging representations administering the resources of the recent republic, the Church in Brazil tended to recover the "organisational model of the Roman Catholic Church" and Bruneau (1979, p. 29) highlights its development as an institution:

"After 1891, the Church started almost from scratch, that is, with only twelve dioceses. By 1900 there were seventeen;

[10] See Thomas Bruneau 1979 p. 23.

[11] Constitution available at http://www.planalto.gov.br/ccivil_03/constituicao/constitui%C3%A7ao91.htm

> in 1910, there were thirty; in 1920, fifty-eight; and in 1964 there were a total of 178 ecclesiastical divisions, which represents an increase of 1,500% in more or less seventy years. It's worth remembering that the bishops appointed to govern these new dioceses were chosen by Rome."

These figures also suggest the position of the Archdiocese of Mariana among the Brazilian episcopate. The Diocese of Mariana was founded in 1745 by Pope Benedict XIV. According to Canon Raymundo Trindade (1953, p. 83), at that time there were only five other bishoprics in the country: Bahia, Rio de Janeiro, Olinda, Maranhão and Pará.

> "Minas, as we have seen, was already quite developed, with 40 parishes and a population totalling 300,000 souls. It was then that Pope Benedict XIV, at the request of King João V, created the Bishopric, with its seat in Marianna, by his MOTU PROPRIO - *Candor lucis atema* - of 6 December 1745."

Trindade (1953, p. 83) also illustrates the congruence between Church and State relations. The author explains the plot in which the then Vila do Ribeirão do Carmo was elevated to city status. Although the Brazilian Church arose in a context of coercion against the Portuguese Court and, later, the Empire, the Roman Church did not allow dioceses to be established on land that was not free or owned by the Church:

> "Previously, the government had given the town of Ribeirão do Carmo the status of a city, a well-deserved honour that no other town could dispute.
> first church in Minas Gerais. In fact, "as the bishops were then nobles of the first magnitude, titular princes, they could not reside, nor did the Pope consent, in Villas, which were not founded on their own lands""

The newspaper O Arquidiocesano appeared during a period in which Brazilian Catholic thought tended to draw closer to the social concerns that emerged from the popular sectors and the middle classes. One of the aims of this work is to identify how the newspaper's position is structured in the aforementioned context, as the official organ of the Archdiocese of Mariana.

> "The new place that Catholicism progressively

occupied in Brazilian society during this period changed its profile both internally and externally [...] Its institutional profile was altered. As a result, the Church's traditional image, language and projection in society took a new direction."[12]

Founded on 29 June 1959, the newspaper "O Arquidiocesano - Órgão Oficial da Arquidiocese de Mariana" (The Archdiocese - Official Organ of the Archdiocese of Mariana), in its first decade of existence, especially in the first seven years, acted as a disseminator of the interests defended by the Catholic Church in relation to the historical-political context then in force in the country.

During this period, the weekly circulated with rare interruptions in cities such as Mariana, Ouro Preto, São João Del Rey, Viçosa, Conselheiro Lafaiete, Juiz de Fora, Ipatinga and Congonhas. For example, it reached 6,000 copies in October 1960. Between 1966 and 1967, there was an intense campaign for 10,000 subscriptions.

The newspaper's first decade falls into the category mentioned by Felipe Pena, in his work "Teoria do Jornalismo" (2008), as Third Journalism: contextualised between 1900 and 1960, it reflected the monopolistic press, highly opinionated, with large print runs and large political sections. In its first year, the newspaper gave more space to doctrinal texts, political opinions and news from the archdiocese. The news consisted of information about the religious calendar of the Archdiocese of Mariana and ecclesiastical activities within the perimeter of the "Archdiocesan Government". They were grouped together in the section labelled "Crónicas da Arquidiocese" (Chronicles of the Archdiocese) from the very first edition. This section remained until 3rd January 1960. Sixteen groups with the same name and similar characteristics were identified by that date. For this reason, they were catalogued at the same time as the other data, even though they didn't fit into any of the three previously established categories. They were catalogued in order to organise these indexes and contribute to future news analyses.

Returning to the national level, although Bruneau (1979, p. 65) highlights

[12] See Ferreira, 2003, p. 98.

the low, almost zero, incidence of social mobilisation groups that confronted the hegemony of the Crown or the authoritarian regime of Getúlio Vargas, the author recognises that the period covered by the analytical corpus of this work is characterised by a rising social concern on the part of some politicians.

> "However, in the period from the late 1950s to 1964 - in Brazil's so-called 'pre-revolution' - there was a growing awareness among various politicians, including President Goulart and many in the opposition, that the institutional obstacles to mobilisation and democratisation had to be removed. The aim was to encourage political participation by mobilising the working classes in urban areas, as well as farmers in rural areas, to change the institutional structure."

While the Vargas regime restored connections in the relationship between church and state that had been lost at the end of the Empire - funding, re-inclusion of religious teaching in schools, among others[13] ; the effervescent instability of the early 1960s represented imminent transformations in Brazilian society, which would later culminate in structural changes in the administrative organisation of the state.

> "Vargas' authoritarian regime protected the Church from the threats to its influence posed by communism, fascism, labour movements, or simple outspoken liberals - all endemic elsewhere during this period. By preserving his own regime, of which the Church was an integral part, he also protected the Church, which in turn supported and legitimised his government."[14]

It is no coincidence that the state structure created by Vargas made political openings difficult in Brazil and therefore represented the maintenance of traditional social structures and the benefits of the classes they protected. However, according to Bruneau, after the Second World War, especially after 1955, Brazilian society also underwent structural changes in the socio-economic spheres.

There was a significant advance in industrialisation which, together with

[13] See Thomas Bruneau: "Religião e politização no Brasil", Edições Loyola, 1979.
[14] See Bruneau, 1979, p. 66

other factors, led to a growing process of urbanisation. Politically, labour movements emerged both in the countryside and in urban areas. In addition, political parties were formed to contest the 1962 elections at all levels.

> "From the order and stability of the previous twenty years (1930-1950), Brazil moved on to instability, disorder and even chaos during the next fifteen years, which culminated in the military coup of 1964."[15]

The social mobilisations that took place during the years in question and the processes of change that developed in Brazil during this specific period threatened the hegemony regained by the Catholic Church during the Vargas era. Among these processes of change, Bruneau (1979, p. 67) states that urbanisation "presaged less attendance at Mass", while there was also a "decrease in vocations and an increase in interest in spiritism and conversions to Protestantism". The author also emphasises the fear that existed in relation to the uncertainties that guided the country's political future.

> "The transformation movements meant that the Church was losing support among the workers, in the student milieu and even in the rural areas where the peasant leagues used religious symbolism to promote structural changes. Most importantly, it wasn't clear to anyone what kind of government would finally take power. If the communists had taken over Cuba, the same could happen in Brazil. The similarities between the Northeast and Cuba were all too obvious and frankly talked about, and the Church was still painfully aware of its losses in Eastern Europe after World War II."

The massive involvement of Catholic institutions in the national political process that culminated in the military coup of 1964 can be seen from publications of the time and by consulting some theorists on the subject, such as historian Carlos Fico (2004), for example, who in "Além do Golpe" (Beyond the Coup) reproduces an article from the newspaper O Globo, of 28 March 1964, about the "Marcha da Família, com Deus, pela liberdade" (March of the Family, with God, for freedom), which took place on the same day. The title of the article was: "In the March of the Family, Rio de Janeiro will express its repudiation of communism". According to Fico, between 19 March

[15] Idem, p. 67

1964 and 8 June of the same year, 51 marches of the same name were held in nine states and the Federal District.

Fico's conceptions of the period leading up to the coup can be confirmed in the newspaper O Arquidiocesano, as Tadeu Pamplona (2008) suggests in his monograph "De Roma a Mariana: Comunismo e Política no 'O Arquidiocesano'(1959-1964)". In his work, Pamplona reproduces an excerpt from an article in "O Arquidiocesano", dated 5 April 1964. The headline read "Brazil, with Rosario in hand, defeated the communist threat".

The National Conference of Bishops of Brazil (CNBB) was founded in 1952 by Bishop Helder Câmara and had, according to Bruneau (1979, p. 70), the aim of "coordinating and unifying the Brazilian Church, which at that time [1950] had more than 110 ecclesiastical units spread across the immense country and had suffered from the lack of a leader since the death of Cardinal Leme". Despite this, Bruneau himself recognises that the CNBB played a more prominent role on the Brazilian scene in the 1960s.

The CNBB arose from an experience of ecclesiastical organisation that was directly influenced by the transformations experienced by the Catholic Church between the 1930s and 1960s: Catholic Action. The movement, officially established in Brazil in 1935, initially sought to reaffirm the Church's teachings in the formation of the society that was being built. After 1950, under a new orientation, Ação Católica Brasileira sought to instruct the lay apostolate in the changes taking place in the Church and to bring it closer to social, artistic and political issues (DELGADO, 2003, 123).

The Archdiocesan was born at a time when the Catholic Church was undergoing changes in various spheres and needed to centralise the Catholic initiative in order to direct religious discourse to the faithful as far as possible. According to Delgado and Passos (2003, p. 123), "the endeavour was to imprint a line that had a more concrete and historical apostolic action. Thus, magazines, bulletins, newspapers, study weeks and courses to train more active and dynamic leaders began to appear".

CHAPTER 2

Transforming units into data: Categorisation

The identification, categorisation, coding and interpretation of the data comprising the analytical *corpus* were developed on the basis of the concepts of Content Analysis found in the homonymous work by Lawrence Bardin (2011) and in the articles by Heloiza Golbspan Herscovitz (LAGO, 2007, p. 123-142) and Wilson Corrêa da Fonseca Júnior (BARROS and DUARTE, 2006, p. 280-303).

Lawrence Bardin (2011, p. 44) states that content analysis "appears as a *set of techniques for analysing communications that uses systematic and objective procedures to describe the content of messages*[16] ". However, the author herself points out that describing the proposed elements is not the main objective of a study based on content analysis techniques. Content analysis builds its results according to the interpretations that can be made from the treatment of coded data.

The results are obtained by relating them to other conclusions previously identified as true. The three reference works on the method used to obtain the data for this research identify the findings caused by the relationship between contents as "inferences" (logical deductions). In the case of O Arquidiocesano, for example, the Archdiocese of São Paulo's acknowledgement of the Catholic Church's contribution to the built environment in Brazil, which culminated in the 1964 civil-military coup, can be considered an index, which, when correlated with other theoretical reference titles (such as Carlos Fico's "Além do Golpe"), acquired the status of truth and was necessary to obtain the inferences that led to the interpretation of the coded data.

According to the New Aurélio Dictionary of the Portuguese Language (2004, p. 1101), inference consists of "passing from premise to conclusion; illation". Also according to the dictionary, the act of inferring is restricted to "drawing by conclusion; deducing by reasoning" (2004, p. 1102). For Bardin (2012, p. 44), "the intention of content analysis is to *infer knowledge about the conditions of production*

[16] Emphasis added.

(or, eventually, reception), an inference that uses indicators (quantitative or not)[17] ".

Wilson Corrêa da Fonseca Júnior (BARROS, 2011, p. 298-299) classifies inference as the "most fertile moment of content analysis, focusing on the implicit aspects of the analysed message". The author divides inferences into two types: specific inferences and general inferences. Specific inferences are restricted to those "linked to the specific situation of the problem being investigated", while general inferences are determined when they overlap with the specific conditions of the analysis, but are of similar importance for understanding the context and conditions of production of the message, which are influential in obtaining the results of the research.

Quoting Klaus Krippendorf (2004), Heloíza Golbspan Herscovitz (BENETTI, p. 128) points out six aspects that should be considered by the researcher in their work: - what are the objects of study; - how are they defined; - what is the universe from which the sample will be drawn; - in what context are the objects of study; - what are the delimitations of the study; and what is the target of the research. To meet these needs, we turned to Bardin (2012, p. 125), who divides the content analysis process into three chronological stages: "pre-analysis, exploration of the material and treatment of the results: inference and interpretation".

2.1 Pre-analysis

For Lawrence Bardin, this stage corresponds to the structural organisation phase of the research. Pre-analysis sets out to establish systems and techniques to guide the research methodology by delimiting and exploring the selected sample within the aspects relevant to the objectives and hypotheses, which are also defined in this phase. The author highlights three objectives of the pre-analysis phase: "the *choice of documents* to be analysed, the formulation of *hypotheses* and *objectives* and the development of indicators to support the final interpretation." (BARDIN, 2012 p. 125).

As termed by Bardin and reiterated by Fonseca Júnior (BARROS, p. 290)

[17] Idem.

and Heloíza Golbspan Herscovitz, "floating reading" can be considered the starting point of content analysis and consists of the first contact between the researcher and the universe of the material to be analysed. Specifically in the case of O Arquidiocesano, when we came across the collections in the Historical Archive of the Mariana City Council - AHCMM and the Ecclesiastical Archive of the Metropolitan Curia of Mariana, we realised the incidence of texts containing themes related to the political context to which Brazil was subjected, especially in the first years of the newspaper's circulation (1959-1967).

In this way, we identified the possibility of submitting this content to processes of analysis that would include both an approach to the frequency with which these texts appear, related to the historical-political context that developed over the decade and with the aim of identifying trends and singularities in Catholic institutional thinking; and characteristics of these texts that would allow us to identify patterns in the discursive line adopted by the newspaper as the official organ of the Archdiocese of Mariana.

Thus, the first objective and hypothesis were determined. It was therefore assumed that the Catholic Church played an important role in the atmosphere in Brazil during the period that coincides with the initial years of the newspaper's foundation. Once we had identified the possibility of collecting a sample of this content that could be subjected to a consolidated analysis, using pre-established techniques for cataloguing and processing the data, we were able to form a theoretical framework, based on authors who dealt with the political participation of the Catholic Church, especially during the 20th century, despite focusing on the history of the Archdiocese of Mariana since its foundation.

The initial aim of this work was to identify how often texts in which the main topic was politics were published, in as many spheres as possible. However, in order to understand which texts would be catalogued and how the categories would be established, it was necessary to delve deeper into the history of the Church's social participation in Brazil and Latin America, as in the work of Enrique Dussel (1989), "História da Igreja Latino-americana (1930 a 1985)"; and of the Church as a whole, seeking to prioritise relations between the Vatican and the Latin Church, when coming across, for example, the work of Thomas Bruneau (1979), "Religião e politização no Brasil".

Both emphasise a worldwide movement to reformulate the Catholic Church, but with specific characteristics for Latin America. However, in order to understand the direction in which these changes were heading, it was necessary to understand the concepts addressed by Paul Richards (1982), in "Morte de las cristandades y nascimento de la Iglesia", in which the author considers the emergence of the Christian Social Doctrine, contextualised by Ildefonso Camacho (1995), with "La doutrina social de la Iglesia: abordagem histórica".

Having noted the importance of the Church's structural reforms in directly influencing the positions adopted by the institution in the Brazilian historical context and, consequently, in the Church's official publications as an organisation, a new objective was developed: to see how often texts were published that indicated, or indicated, issues relating to the Catholic Church's basic reforms, especially in the time frame of the research.

As this is an investigation into a probable representation[18] of the Catholic Church's positions as an institution with a broad hierarchy, especially on issues with a direct impact on the current social (dis)order, it was deemed necessary to formulate another objective: to catalogue all the texts in which the newspaper's discourse of self-representation predominates, in other words, those in which the newspaper uses to talk about itself, such as: raising subscriptions, graces achieved and valuing the Catholic press, for example.

In order to make the syntactic-temporal cut of the documents to be processed and therefore make up the analytical *corpus* of the work, Bardin (2012, p. 126-131), cited later by Fonseca Júnior (p. 292-294), establishes rules that must be obeyed to guarantee the scientific bias of the sampling selection process.

The first rule cited by Bardin (2012, p. 126) is the "rule of completeness", in

[18] See Patric Charaudeau, in Media Discourse, 2006.

which "you can't leave out any of the elements for this or that reason", in other words, when defining the *corpus*, you need to know about all the elements that make it up, previously identified as relevant to the analysis. It was therefore decided that the *corpus* of this study would be the first eight years of circulation of O Arquidiocesano, corresponding to the 405 editions published during this period.

After the exhaustiveness rule, the "representativeness rule" must be obeyed. In the specific case of this work, we opted for a selection of materials that could indicate representations or positions capable of contributing to deductions about the Catholic Church's role in the society in question and that met the proposed objectives. For this reason, all the editions were checked and the texts that met any of the aforementioned objectives were coded. According to Wilson Corrêa da Fonseca Júnior (p. 293), these decisions about the *corpus* are decisive in defining the emphasis to be given to the research.

> "If the amount of material to be analysed is very large, it will be necessary to adopt statistical procedures in order to obtain an overall view, and you should opt for quantitative analysis. In this case, you gain breadth but lose depth. If the aim is to delve deeper into the content, it will be impossible to process a large amount of data and a qualitative analysis will have to be carried out".

Despite looking for criteria that emphasise the hybridity of the method, the quantitative aspects of content analysis were given greater prominence. This does not mean that the latent criteria of the analysis were discarded. The recording and context units, explained below, try to deduce the implicit aspects of the messages uttered by the vehicle.

Because all the elements catalogued are part of the same universe and correlate in order to achieve the proposed objectives, this work also complies with the third rule cited by Bardin and Fonseca Júnior: *"the rule of homogeneity"*. This rule was used with the aim of obtaining global results, as well as comparing the individual results of each category. The overall results found were the incidence rates for each category over the months and then the years. The individual results correspond to the relationship between the categories in the same historical context. Based on this processed data, inferences were drawn and then the information was interpreted.

The coded data complies with the fourth rule cited by Bardin and Fonseca Júnior, as it comes from the same universe (a complete collection of the 34 years the newspaper O Arquidiocesano has been published), corresponds to the same time frame (eight years of continuous publications) and was subjected to the same analysis procedures.

2.2 Coding

According to Fonseca Júnior (BARROS, p. 294), "coding is the process of transforming raw data in a systematic way, according to rules of enumeration, aggregation and classification, with the aim of enlightening the analyst about the characteristics of the selected material". After the pre-analysis process, in which the topic to be researched was established, the hypotheses and objectives were formulated, a theoretical framework was adopted and the analytical *corpus* was cut out, the recording units were defined.

The recording units were developed based on the themes that guided the development of the objectives in the pre-analysis phase. They correspond to political participation; self-representation; and, finally, the reforms that have taken place in the institution, which can be seen in the pages of the newspaper. These units led to the creation of coding and analysis categories. Bardin (2012, p. 133) values the "nuclei of meaning" in this theme and discards the cataloguing of forms.

> "The theme, as a recording unit, corresponds to a cutting rule (of meaning and not of form) that is not provided, since the cutting depends on the level of analysis and not on regulated formal manifestations."

The registration units therefore consist of the headlines that include the representative discourses of the newspaper, within the scope of the aforementioned objectives, subdivided into three primary cataloguing categories. These make up the sampling units, delimited here by the newspaper editions. These editions, in turn, make up the *corpus of* the analysis, which also acts as a factor in representing the universe of known documents. This structure can be understood from the figure below.

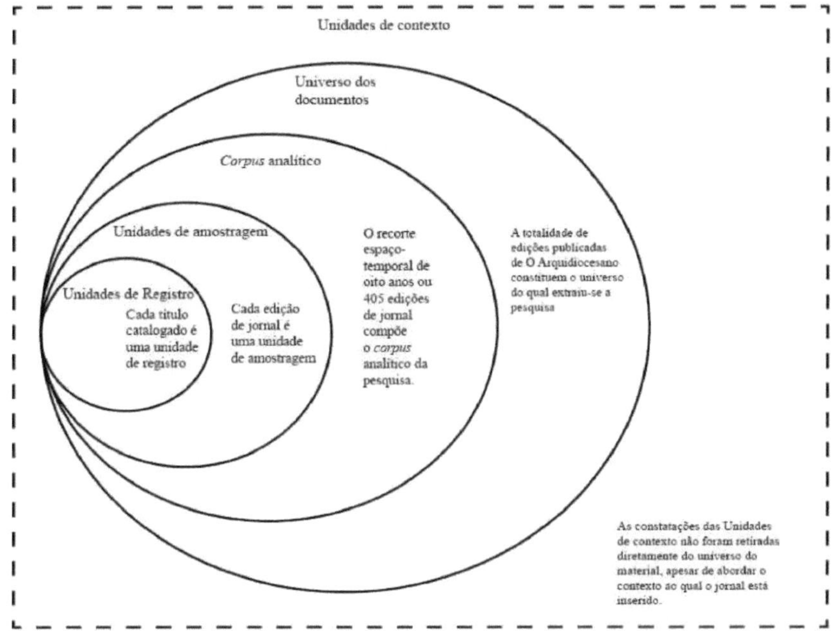

In order to understand the units of record, it was also necessary to establish units of context, which contribute to setting the content in the historical context that is the reference for the analytical approach. To this end, in addition to the inferences drawn in Chapter 1, we sought to understand the structures in place when the Archdiocesan Church was founded.

From this and other data, it was possible to construct the first table for structuring the analysis, based on the criteria suggested by the Alfredo de Carvalho Network for identifying newspapers, which can be seen below.

I- GENERAL DATA

Journal title	□ Archdiocesan - Official organ of the Archdiocese of Mariana
Analysis period	t05 issues from the first eight years of circulation
Collection where it was found	• Archive of the Metropolitan Curia of the Archdiocese of Mariana

	• Mariana City Council Historical Archive
Conservation - Paper - Microfilm	Paper (annual books)

GRAPHIC ASPECTS

Format (in centimetres)	Spot: 0.4 Im x 0.29m
Number of pages • In the first issue • In subsequent editions (sampling)	- 06 pages - 04 pages
SUPPLEMENTS	Not broken down in the period covered by the analytical corpus
NOTEBOOK	Not broken down in the period covered by the analytical corpus

III - LOCATION

PRINTING PLACE(S) Address - Name of bookshop, printer, shop Single sale?	Archdiocesan Printing Office Subscriptions only (in the editions)
DISTRIBUTOR Distributor name	Not available

IV - PERIODICITY

First number (day, month and year)	29 June 1959
Last issue (day, month and year)	18th June 1967
Period of publication (indicate interruptions)	Interruptions: • Between 29/06/1959 and 16/08/1959; • Between 16/08/1959 and 30/08/1959; • Between 13/09/1959 and 27/09/1959.
Frequency	WEEKLY
Total annual editions	Year I: 40 Year II: 52

	Year III: 52 Year IV: 53 YearV: 52 Year VI: 52 Year VII: 52 Year VIII: 52

V - COMMERCIALISATION

Print run (stated in the editions)	5,000 (from issue 27, 20/03/1960). 5,300 (appears from issue 50, 28/8/1960) 5,600 (appears from issue 56, 09/10/1960) 6,000 (appears from issue 59, 30/10/1960) Not explicit in the masthead from issue 155, 02/09/1962
Other sources of funding • Private support • Public support	Not listed, only Graces Reached (donations from the faithful in gratitude)

VI-GENERAL EDITORIAL ASPECTS

Main sections	Sections are not explicitly defined
Main editorials	There is no explicit division of editorials.
Are there letter sections? Name of this section	Suggested since issue number 1, under the name "Readers write to us".
Do you publish photos?	Yes
Most frequent type of news (political, economic, police, etc.)	Information on the Archdiocese's actions, commitments and events in the parishes it covers.
Type of texts published (news, chronicles, commentaries, pamphlets, etc.)	Political items, religious instructions, information on the activities of the clergy. News with a high degree of opinion.
Historical events (historical episodes broadcast prominently)	Death of Pope John XXIII, of Archbishop Helvécio Gomes, the 1964 coup, the Second Vatican Council, among others.

VII - EDITORIAL ASPECTS OF THE FRONT PAGE

Do you edit headlines?	Edits headlines and uses subheads. Headlines are overemphasised in

Format (colour po, subheadline)	relation to the body of the text.
Do you edit photos?	Sporadically.
Edit another type of image	He publishes illustrations, cartoons and lithographs.
Journal logo Do you have a logo? Yes or no?	No logo.
Slogan Publish a slogan or motto? Which one?	It has no slogan.
Do you edit calls?	Occasionally, but without an aesthetic pattern.
Do front-page stories remain on the inside pages?	The articles continue on the previous pages and, occasionally, are continued in subsequent editions.

VIII - JOURNALISTS (please indicate names where appropriate)

Owner(s)	Metropolitan Curia of the Archdiocese of Mariana
Director(s)	Until 1960: Canon Pedro Terra After 1960: Canon José Geraldo Vidigal de Oak Under the guidance of Archbishop Oscar de Oliveira
Editor-in-chief	Not available
Editors	Not specified
Main collaborators	Not specified
Editors/reporters	Not specified

IX-CONCLUSIONS

GENERAL COMMENTS Synthetic references relevant to vehicle history	Established during a period of imminent reform in the Catholic Church. It is important to identify aspects of this change in the newspaper's publications.
EXPLICIT INSTITUTIONAL LINKS Is the vehicle linked to a particular institution or was it politically linked to	Official organ of the Archdiocese of Mariana • It has an institutional character

any group?	• Strong political participation • Doctrinal character

Once these elements had been defined, it was finally possible to draw up the fields of analysis to which all the selected content would be subjected. The data was catalogued with the help of a digital spreadsheet that allowed analysis criteria to be added after cataloguing the sample, whenever the need arose to subdivide the categories or expand the information catalogued about the data obtained. Thus, the initial heading for defining the fields can be established, reserving a folder for each year of the newspaper's circulation, as shown in the following spreadsheet.

	A	B	C	D	E	F	G	H	I	J	K
1	Edição	Data	Título	Autor	Categoria	Página	Manchete	Continuação no interior	Tiragem	Série	Observações
2											
3											
4											
5											
6											
7											
8											
9											
10											
11											
12											
13											
14											
15											
16											

2.3 Categorisation

According to Bardin (2012 p. 147), "*categorisation* is an operation of classifying elements of a set by differentiating them and then regrouping them according to genre (analogy), using previously defined criteria". The author considers categories to be classes capable of grouping units of records, in this case the headlines, based on predefined criteria of similarity. In order to define the categories used to analyse this work, we opted for the semantic approach of distributing the texts into categories.

> "The categorisation *criterion* can be *semantic* (thematic categories: for example, all the themes that mean anxiety are grouped under the category 'anxiety', while those that mean relaxation are grouped under the conceptual heading 'relaxation'), syntactic (verbs, adjectives), lexical (classification of words according to their meaning, with pairings of synonyms and close meanings) and expressive (for example, categories that classify the various language disorders)."

The first objective of categorisation is, according to Bardin (2012 p. 148), "to provide, by condensation, a simplified representation of the raw data". In order to do this, the fields A, B, C, D, F and I were initially established, which correspond to the edition, date, title, author, page and print run respectively. In this way, any title can be localised if some of these fields are known, such as the edition and/or date, for example.

Defining categorisation as a "structuralist process", Bardin subdivides it into two stages: *inventory* and *classification.* In the inventory phase, the delimitation of the aforementioned fields helps to isolate the elements according to the chronological order in which the titles appear. During the classification phase, the definition of analysis categories separates the recording units according to the predominant theme in the selected titles.

To carry out this process, the system of categories was developed and the titles were separated as best as possible as the elements were found, as suggested by Lawrence Bardin (2012 p. 149). In this way, the organisation of the material is conditioned to the impressions made during the floating reading and the composition of the theoretical framework, thus reducing the possibility of new categories appearing during the cataloguing process.

In the opinion of Bardin (2012, p. 149-150), later quoted by Fonseca Júnior (BARROS, 2011, p. 298), good categorisation must meet five requirements. The first of these is "mutual exclusion", in which an element included in one category cannot simultaneously be included in another. The second characteristic, called "homogeneity", reiterates that only recording units of the same nature can be included in the same category. Relevance" is the third characteristic defended by the author. She states that the system developed for categorisation must "reflect the intentions of the investigation". In the fourth category mentioned, "objectivity and fidelity" are valued. For the author, the procedures must be objective in order to guarantee the fidelity of the results and enable possible repetition of the analysis. In the last quality defended by Bardin, "productivity", the results provided must be rich in "inferences, data and new hypotheses".

The process of categorising the analytical *corpus* extracted from the universe of O Arquidiocesano led to the titles being divided into three semantic groups: politics, self-representation/propaganda and institutional reform of the Church. The indexes for this work, however, were only generated for the categories "politics" and "reform", as both are related in the formation of the desired inferences. The texts referring to the newspaper's self-propaganda were categorised under the same organisational codes as the others, with the subsequent aim of analysing aspects of identity and representation present in the discourse of these messages.

2.3.1 Category 1: Politics

The first category determined in this research aimed to catalogue and identify titles that addressed issues related to the national political context. Within this category, subdivisions were established that make up the "Politics" code, according to the perception of patterns and differences within this theme. They were established according to the depth of the research.

In the first year of circulation of O Arquidiocesano, between 21 June 1959 and 19 June 1960, 69 titles were catalogued that could be classified into the previously defined categories. Of these 69, fifteen had politics as their main theme. In this section, two main semantic patterns were identified, which consequently led to two subcategories: Freemasonry and Communism.

Of the fifteen titles related to politics in the first year of O Arquidiocesano, a series of six articles entitled "Why the Church condemns Freemasonry" stands out. This series, signed by J. Caprile, circulated between issues 2 and 7 and is considered political because organisations like the Freemasons represented threats to the Church's hegemony, as did communism and popular revolts. Another similarity found in the category is the negative nature of the messages in both subcategories.

When cataloguing the texts on communism, it emerged that the first publication on the subject took place on 6 September 1959, in the newspaper's fourth edition. The text entitled "Comunismo em 3 tempos" (Communism in 3 times) is signed by Father Dr Belchior Comélio, who was responsible for 12 texts in the first year of O Arquidiocesano's life, on various topics. After that, another fourteen publications in the first year dealt with communist themes. Father Dr Belchior Comélio da Silva signed two more texts during this period on the subject of communism.

Thus, the graph of the incidence of texts that could be classified under category 1, "Politics", and subdivided between the two subcategories during year I of circulation, can be seen as follows:

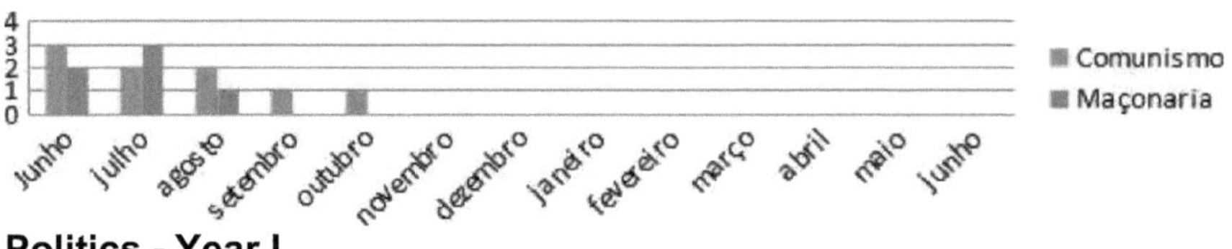

Politics - Year I

In this first year, therefore, there was a low incidence of texts dealing with political issues that could be included in the categories analysed. There was only a small regular incidence between August and October 1959. It can be said, however, that the theme of "communism", despite not being grouped into a series (as is the case with the articles in the subcategory "freemasonry"), appears over a longer period of time, which may indicate a constant concern with this theme at different times/contexts in year I.

While only 69 entries were catalogued in the first year, year II, which begins with the 29 June 1960 issue, contributed 180 titles to this analysis, divided between the three categories. For the "politics" category, 69 texts were recorded.

Making up an absolute majority, disagreements with communist theories and practices were the most evident. This is clear from the very first issues. Issue 45 (the fifth of that year), of 24 July 1960, began a series in which the front page headline was entitled "Communism Aims to Conquer Cuba", in the two subsequent issues. The series warns of a possible threat of communist invasion in other Latin American countries as well.

Of the 69 titles selected, only five do not correspond to the theme of communism. The subcategories formed were "communism" and "other". In this case, the annual monitoring chart for the second year of circulation developed as follows:

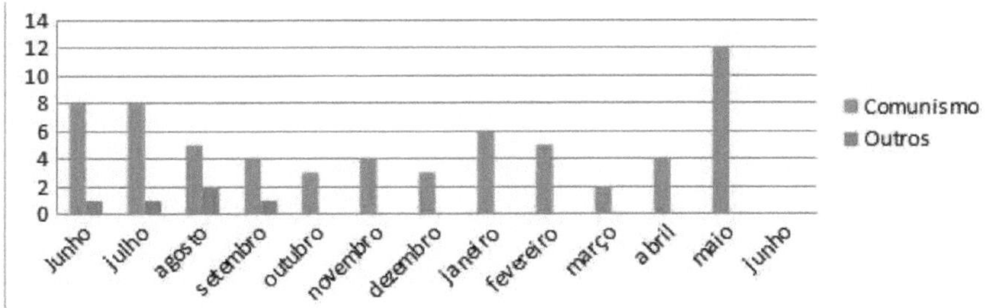

Politics - Year II

In this graph, the hegemony of discourses against communism is evident, overlapping with other themes related to politics. In each of the months of June, November and April, there is a codified article dealing with other political aspects. The first article, from 29 June 1960, covers the political participation of the Catholic Action movement, while the article from 20 November, loaded with ufanistic characteristics, suggests changes to the Brazilian flag, even supposing the existence of the phrase "Order and Progress" on a national flag to be a pleonasm. The articles published in January that do not fall into the "communism" category are signed by Bishop Luis Mousinho, then bishop of Ribeirão Preto, and are entitled "Rectitude in Politics" and "It is up to Catholics to be better citizens". Both call for greater effective participation by Catholics in the country's political structures. Finally, the April article seeks to direct the Church's actions in the trade unions.

The first text added to the "communism" subcategory, signed by Cónego Adalberto Damasceno, was entitled "Speaking badly is easy" and ran in issue 42 on 3 July 1960. As well as defending the authorities and, therefore, the current order, the text alludes to the climate of instability that was forming in Brazilian society, as can be seen in the first few lines:

> "There is discontent in all social classes and professions. Recriminations against those who govern, against the ecclesiastical and military authorities, now it's the President of the Republic, there it's the Governor of the State, here it's the Bishop of the Diocese, the Vicar of the Parish, there it's the Municipal Mayor, further on it's the State and Municipal Chambers, the Federal Parliament. No-one escapes the hammer of the people, who are always dissatisfied and angry. The spirit of indiscipline

> has invaded homes, temples, schools, houses of religious formation, even... Who can stop the macabre march of daily events?"
>
> (The Archdiocesan, no. 42, p. 4, 03/07/1960)

From issue 45 onwards, boxes with the title "COMMUNISM" also appeared alongside the headline on the front pages. The first, supposedly signed by Rui Barbosa, states that "Communism is not fraternity: it is the invasion of hatred between the classes. It is not the reconciliation of man; it is his mutual extermination...". From 30 July 1960, the newspaper also uses quotes from Pope Pius XI on the subject of communism. In issue 50, of 28 August 1960, the text quoted deals with the issue of women in communism.

> "For communism in particular, there is no bond that ties women to the family and the domestic home. Proclaiming the principle of the emancipation of women, it removes them from domestic life and from caring for their offspring, in order to bring them into public life and collective activities, to the same extent as men, passing on to the community the loss of their home and children. In short, parents are denied the right to education, which is considered to be the exclusive right of the community, in whose name and by commission alone parents can exercise it."
>
> (The Archdiocesan, no. 50, p. 3, 28 August 1960)

On 18 September, in issue 53, another series of front-page headlines began, this time entitled "A Cry of Alarm Against Red Proselytism". In this series, signed by Father Ricardo Lombardi, there is concern about alleged Russian recruitment of young people. In the first text, the author claims that a university has been set up in Moscow for students from Africa and Latin America, with the aim of bringing them into the "USSR's campaign for cultural and ideological penetration of the world". The last paragraph of the second text in this series suggests ways of resisting this "danger", although it concludes with a warning to readers.

> "For the comfort of those who still hold young people in high esteem, we will say that the work of enchantment does not always fulfil its intended purpose. Looking at the news obtained from authorised sources, there have also been cases of firm and

> courageous resistance in the name of freedom, against the thick Marxist propaganda. But what do these few cases mean in the face of the general danger? Can one allow a public fountain of infected water to be opened, consoling oneself that there is a pharmacy nearby?"
>
> (The Archdiocesan, no. 53, p. 2, 18/09/1960)

The graph for year II also shows a jump in the number of titles on communism in the last month analysed. While the months of July and August 1960 each registered a maximum of eight texts on communism, in June 1961 there were 12 texts on the subject, not including the issue of 29 June 1961, which is part of the graph for year III (1961-1962). In the issue of 4 June 1961 alone, six texts were catalogued. The main reason for this higher incidence, compared to previous periods, may be the dioceses' holding of public conferences on communism, about which there were two articles in this issue alone.

The cataloguing indexes for the newspaper's third year of circulation suggest an increase in political publications by the Catholic institution. While 69 titles falling into this category were registered in the previous year, 216 were registered the following year, subdivided into two subcategories. This corresponds to approximately 62 per cent of all those coded in the year in question. A total of 347 titles were catalogued.

The subjects covered in relation to politics are, in short, communism, land reform and elections. Despite the need to redistribute these texts into subcategories, the titles were only included in the "Communism" subcategory. This choice was based on two main aspects.

The first of these is the undisputed supremacy of texts in which communism is directly addressed, which exceeds 90 per cent in relation to titles dealing with other political themes. The second reason refers to the intentionality of the content. Both the publications on land reform and those on the elections were motivated by the anti-communist campaign.

On 5 November 1960, the Archdiocesan began a series entitled "Agrarian Reform", made up of front-page headlines on the subject. The topic was categorised under the subcategory "communism" based on indices, such as the content used, for example, in the third paragraph of the series' opening text, when it states that "emphatically proclaiming the division of land would be a simplistic measure that, far from solving, would aggravate problems. What would be the point of distributing land to those who couldn't or wouldn't cultivate it properly?". In this excerpt, we can see the fear of the measures advocated by the Federal Government to promote a greater division of assets concentrated in the countryside, supposedly aligned with communist practices. This opposition between the Agrarian Reform proposed by the Church and that supposedly proposed by communism can also be exemplified in the third paragraph of the thirteenth text in this series, published in issue 124, of 28 January 1962:

> "In the minds of communists and socialists, Agrarian Reform has a revolutionary sense of confusionism. In the minds of those who really want the good of society, it means promoting the common good of landowners and workers in the countryside, in accordance with justice and charity."
> (The Archdiocesan, no. 124, p. 1, 28/01/1962)

On the subject of elections, two texts were published in issue 93 of 25 June 1961, the first issue of that year. The first was signed by a movement called the "Confederation of Christian Families". In this text, entitled "Electoral Alliance for the Family", although it doesn't explicitly mention communism, the message reiterates that it obeys the laws of the Church. The second text in this issue helps to legitimise the permanence of the previous one in the aforementioned subcategory. Entitled "Unofficialisation of the Communist Party", the text appears in the "Archdiocesan Government" section.

In the previous two years of the newspaper's circulation, this section was used to publicise official communications from the Archdiocese, such as appointments, legislations and decisions from the top to the clergy. Thus, by including a doctrinal text to the faithful about communism in a section intended for official communications, the intention to publish the first text is clear, in which the message guarantees obedience to the institution's determinations.

Among the publications included in the "communism" subcategory, the series of cartoons "Behind the Iron Curtain" appeared in issue 113, dated 12 November 1961. Between 12 November 1961 and 8 April 1962, sixteen cartoons of the same name were catalogued.

The cartoons usually consist of four frames and are staged by a child and a communist soldier. In this first text, the communist soldier opens a hole in the ice to fish and, as a result, hooks the devil. Although they don't follow the conventional textual structure, divided into sentences and paragraphs, the cartoons establish a direct language with the interlocutors, which is easy to understand and divided into periods.

Some editions of that year's circulation stood out for their predominance of political texts, which intensified from January 1962 onwards. Of particular note is issue 122, dated 14 January, in which all nine of the catalogued record units refer to communism. If the month of January is analysed as a single sampling unit, the incidence of political texts among all those catalogued exceeds 86%. In May of the same year, there were twenty-three entries in the political category, with an incidence rate of over 88%. Also noteworthy are the rates recorded in June 1962, which account for twenty units of records, even though it doesn't contain the twenty-fourth June 1962 issue, determined by the way it was archived as the first of year IV. The incidence of political texts over the months of the third year of circulation of O Arquidiocesano can be seen in the graph:

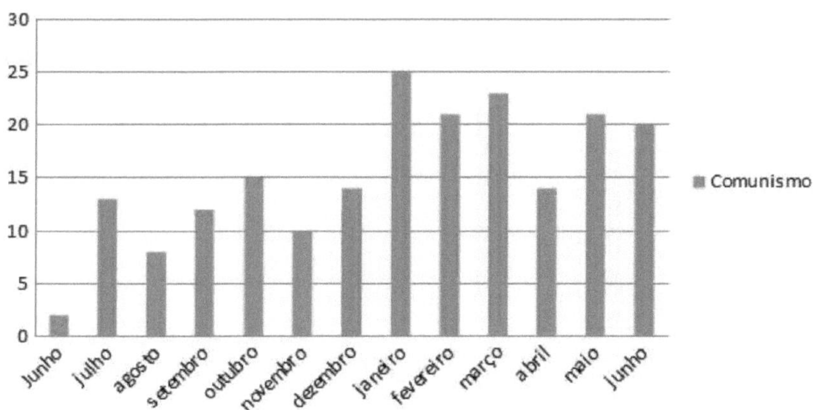

YEAR III-Politics

As mentioned in the previous paragraph, the fourth year of circulation of the newspaper O Arquidiocesano began on 24 June 1962. In this issue, number 145, another textual structure is used to express the paper's repudiation of communist ideology. The newspaper uses an endnote on page three, signed by G. Tiberghein, which says: ""Materialism not only eliminates freedom, it strikes with the same blow the ideal, progress, reason, all the laws of moral life"".

That year, 176 titles corresponding to the "politics" category were catalogued. Once again, the themes of "communism" and "elections" were predominant. However, this time it was necessary to divide them into subcategories due to the high incidence of texts covering both themes, despite the fact that some titles related to elections also mention aspects of communism. There were also texts that did not address these issues directly and therefore deserved to be catalogued in another subcategory.

Thus, the subcategories established to code the texts related to politics were: "communism", "elections" and "other". Once again, the subcategory "communism" garnered the largest number of texts. There were 132 publications that year and the highest number of texts was between February and April 1963. The subcategory "elections" received 38 publications, concentrated mainly between July and October 1962. In the "other" subcategory, only six publications were coded in the entire year of circulation.

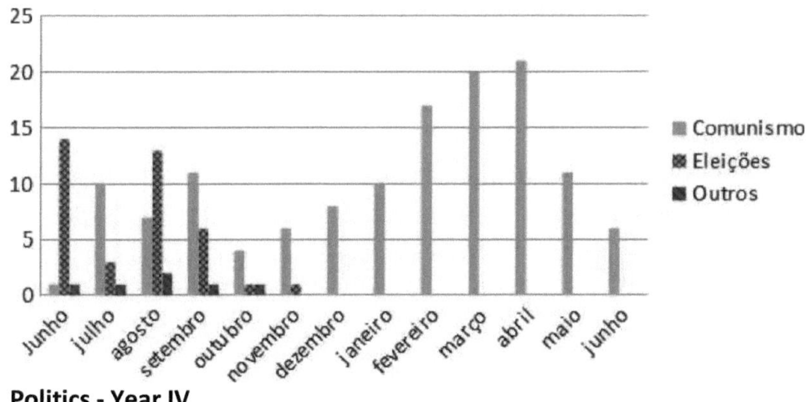

Politics - Year IV

The incidence of texts on the subject of elections stands out because it illustrates the media outlet's direct political participation in the elections that took place on 7 October 1962. The first article that falls into this subcategory appears in issue 147, on the first day of July 1962, and is entitled "RULES to follow when choosing a candidate". In this article, as in five others in the same month, there is a hat with the words: "ELECTORAL ALLIANCE FOR THE FAMILY". In another article, published on 2 September of the same year, it is also possible to see the effective role of the Catholic movement in the electoral process:

> "On 27 July, the Electoral Alliance for the Family submitted a request to the Superior Electoral Court asking that Carlos Prestes' request for the legalisation of the Communist Party in Brazil be rejected."

The paper also uses end-of-page notes to indoctrinate the faithful about voting, as suggested by the one on page four of the issue 157, dated 16 September 1962: "Voting is a sacred duty. Catholics cannot, without sinning, vote for **communist** or **socialist** candidates. Even if these candidates deny it in their words, they confirm it by their tendencies or attitudes." This note is repeated in the following four editions, also on page four.

Another way of understanding the intentionality of the publications on the subject of the elections is to catalogue the registration units for the month of October

1962. All the texts from that month on this subject were taken from issue 160, on 7 October 1962 - the day of the elections. On page four alone, there are four texts covered by this subcategory.

The headline on the page, entitled ""Votes belong to the patrimony of the fatherland"" has the subtitle: "ELECTORAL ALLIANCE FOR THE FAMILY releases new list of candidates approved by it." The article entitled "TODAY!" points out seven topics in the first person with guidelines for voting. Topics 3 and 7 stand out among them:

> "3 - Divorcists and philo-communists won't get my vote.
> [---]
> 7 - Politicians with their hands out who want to turn our homeland into another Cuba orbiting the red planet of hatred and blood will have my disapproval, never my vote."

The first text to fall into the "other" category is also in issue 146. The title of this article is "President Goulart praises Cardinal Motta". Despite dealing with the issue of agrarian reform and politics directly, the article addresses issues that are close to the reforms that took place in the Catholic Church in the historical-contextual period in which these documents were analysed and which were responsible for the emergence of analysis category number three.

Two other texts that fall into this category were published in issues 154 and 155, on 26 August and 2 September 1962 respectively. Both, signed by Father Edmundo H. Dreher, S. J., are entitled "The civic duty of Catholics" and address, as their main theme, the date of seven September, as "Fatherland Day". The other two texts appear only in February and April 1963.

Although there was a slight reduction in the gross number of political publications in the fifth year of circulation of O Arquidiocesano, the content it published represented an exacerbated polarisation between Catholic thought and what was supposedly proposed by communist ideologies. The peculiarity of this period is evident when the civil-military coup took place in April 1964, in which the environment formed in Brazilian society culminated in a rupture of the political structure in force in the country under the government of João Goulart.Possibly for this reason, only the subcategory "communism" was formed in relation to the category "politics". There were 122 titles in this category, fifty-four fewer than the previous year. In addition to the different content of these texts, the relationship between the incidences each month can favour an understanding of the climate of instability that formed throughout the year of circulation.

It is worth noting that two texts from the 14 July 1963 edition were taken from this category. In the first of these, the headline on page four, the newly-elected Pope Paul VI greets Brazil in the person of President João Goulart. On the same page there is a reply from the president stating that he believes in the Pope's teachings for the Brazilian nation.

The incidence of texts involving communism fluctuated between the months of 1963. However, from January 1964 onwards there was a gradual increase in the number of entries in this category until April. The titles catalogued only between February and April 1964 represent around 42% of those coded in this category for that year.

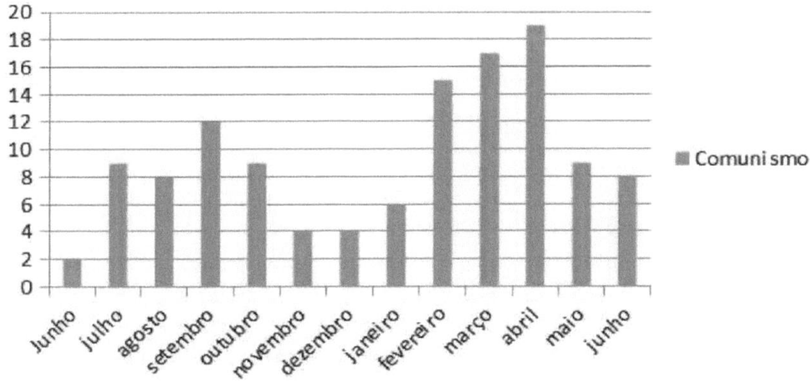

YEAR V - Politics

Issue 238 of O Arquidiocesano, dated 5 April 1964, i.e. the first after the symbolic milestone of the military seizure of power, explores the theme of communism with a large majority of other subjects. Of the thirteen catalogued in this issue, ten fall into this category. Three texts were catalogued on the front page alone. In addition, the headlines on pages two, three and four also deal with this issue. Page four also features an illustration in which a projectile is surrounded by a third in the shape of a map of Brazil. On the projectile, the word "Peace" is written in Latin (PAX) .[19]

With regard to the coup, issue 240 of 19 April 1964 stands out. In this issue, the headlines on pages three and four discuss the military intervention. The title of the first article is "And that's what Jango didn't believe..." and the first paragraph exalts religious participation in the tensions that culminated in the coup:

> "It was the rosary that beat him. The rosary of the fragile hands of the women of Minas Gerais, who expelled him from the Health Department. The rosary of five hundred thousand people from São Paulo and a million from Rio de Janeiro in the most beautiful processions this Christian country has ever seen. In those two long parades, between the chimneys of the power plants that are the pride of our work, and by the sea, in the city that is the glory of nature and the honour of our civilisation. He went to the Rosary, prayed loudly in the squares and streets, in chapels and temples. Murmured on our knees in the family, in front of the oratory around the supper table."
>
> (The Archdiocesan, no. 240, p. 3, 19/04/1964)

The headline on page four of this issue is entitled "Brazil, with Rosario in hand, defeated the communist invasion". There is also a headline: "New Lepanto, Uncrucial, Saves the American Continent". The article is divided into sub-headings. Under the subheading "THE COMMUNIST PENETRATION", the newspaper attacks the deposed government, accusing it of the official bodies being run by communists.

> "Brazil was in fact on top of a volcano.
>
> Federal bodies, ministries, autarchies, institutes, Petrobras, Supra, student organisations, trade unions, etc. were left in a state of chaos throughout Brazil. Their directors and presidents disappeared, fled or were arrested, confirming that the key points were in the hands of the communists. Numerous deposits of subversive material were swept up, a sign that, in fact, it was known where everything was to be found, only that there was no superior disposition to 'discover' them."
>
> (The Archdiocesan, no. 240, p. 3, 19/04/1964)

[19] Illustration attached.

In the next edition, published on 26 April 1964, there is an article reproduced from O Estado de Minas, signed by Alberto Deodato, from 3 April 1964. The title of the article is "Warning to Brazilian politicians". The article suggests that the military intervention took place to re-establish democracy in Brazil. After this publication, the incidence of texts related to communism resumed the oscillation seen in the first half of the year. The sixth year of circulation of O Arquidiocesano began with issue 250, of June 1964. That year saw a decline in the number of publications in the "politics" category. Forty-four registration units were catalogued, subdivided into two other categories: thirty-two titles in the "communism" subcategory and twelve titles in the "other" subcategory. The indexes catalogued over the months can be seen below.

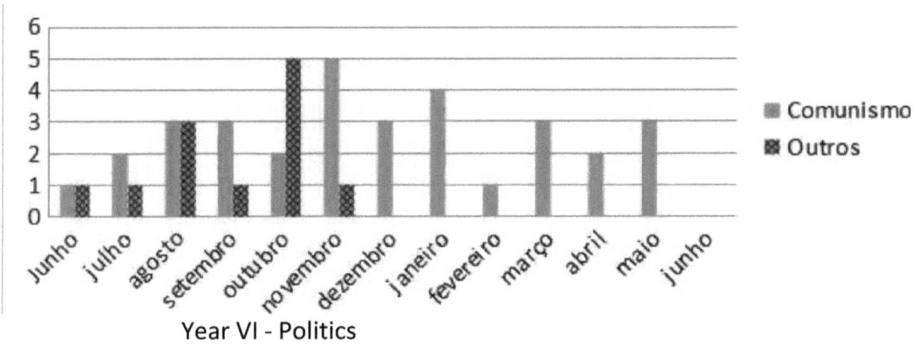

Among the "other" texts, there are titles about the Homeland and Bandeira, as a priority, as well as a text about a visit by the governor of Minas Gerais to Mariana, on the occasion of the Basilica's Feast Day; and another title about a spiritual retreat for parliamentarians from Minas Gerais.

Among the publications on communism, the headline of issue 276, of 27 December 1964, signed by the Archbishop of Mariana, Dom Oscar de Oliveira, and entitled "Necessary Revolution", stands out. Calling it a "white revolution", Dom Oscar classifies the coup as the "greatest event of 1964", because without bloodshed it was "promising tranquillity". In an article from 14 February 1965, entitled "I'm back in everything", author José Clemente states that a revolution was necessary to restore order.

Also noteworthy is the headline on the fourth page of issue 292, entitled "Brazil's Christian Trajectory". On 18 April 1965, O Arquidiocesano published a prayer said in the Carmo Church in Ouro Preto, "on the occasion of the first anniversary of the MARCH REVOLUTION".

In the newspaper's seventh year of circulation, fifty-four titles were devoted to the "politics" category. Once again, the theme of "communism" was predominant. Content referring to this theme was catalogued forty-one times, which corresponds to around 75% of the registration units that make up the category. Among the other titles catalogued in this category, there are texts about reforms to the tax system and the Civil Code, as well as themes involving issues related to the homeland. Although this is a low incidence of content, these texts are not related to the theme of the previous subcategory and it was therefore necessary to subdivide the "politics" category into two others: "communism" and "others".

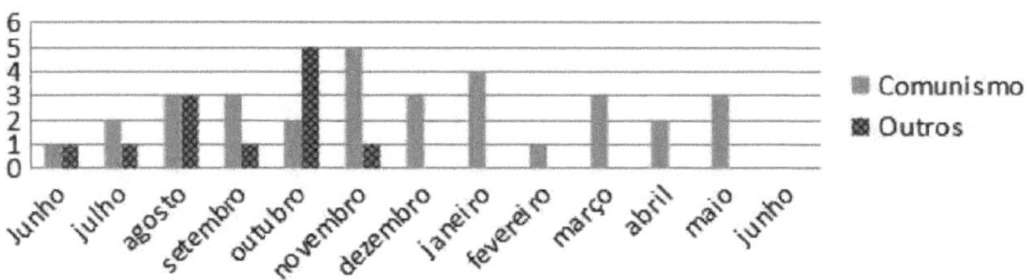

Politics - Year VII

The texts in the first subcategory continue to disseminate opinions contrary to communist ideology. What is happening, however, is that the newspaper is updating the way it disseminates this content. After the civil-military coup of 1964, the messages are predisposed to reiterate that the communist threat still exists, even though the "revolution" was responsible for the return of tranquillity to the country. This can be seen in the two articles in issue 317, dated 10 October 1965. Both on the front page, the first, a correspondence from Paris, is entitled "Communism doesn't give up on Brazil". The second article, from Rio de Janeiro, deals with the "New Communist plans for the conquest of Brazil". Also noteworthy in the following issue is the headline on page three, entitled "Dialogue No, Confrontation Yes!", supposedly sent from Vatican City.

The last graph generated, which looks at the incidence of texts related to politics over the months, refers to the eighth year of circulation of O Arquidiocesano. As expected, the theme of "communism" once again led to the generation of the subcategory of the same name. In short, the texts resemble the patterns seen in the previous year of reaffirming the existence of the communist threat. The data recorded corresponds to the lowest incidence of recording units.

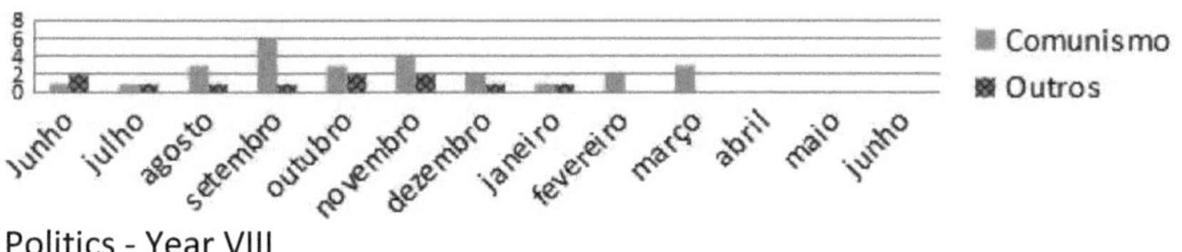

Politics - Year VIII

On the subject of communism, texts were highlighted that were concerned with reaffirming that it was impossible for Catholicism to align itself with communist practices, as suggested by the headline on page three of issue 364, of 4 September 1966, entitled "Conciliar attitude is opposed to 'Conciliarism'". On the same page, there is also a text signed by Fr Deolindo Coelho, which deals with the actions of the military government. The article is entitled "*Empty* stomachs, sources of revolts".

> "The Revolutionary Government, if it doesn't want to become more and more unpopular because of the drastic (necessary) measures it is adopting, should turn its sights to agriculture. Hungry stomachs are the source of revolts. Barbacena, August 1966".

The predominant themes of the texts that did not directly address communism were once again patriotic issues and criticisms of the civil code, as well as the implementation of the new currency, the Cruzeiro Novo. Thirty-seven record units were coded in the "politics" category, subdivided into "communism" - twenty-six units - and "others" - eleven titles.

2.3.2 Category 2: Reform

The composition of this category arose from the need to understand the development of Catholic thought disseminated through its official communication organs. This need arose, above all, after reading the collection and confirming the theoretical framework in studies such as those by Ildefonso Camacho, Pablo Richards and Scott Maiwanring.

The "Reformation" category should include headlines referring to changes in ecclesiastical guidelines covered by the newspaper during the research period. In order to catalogue this material, the category needed to be subdivided into three semantic filters.

At the same time as there were texts suggesting an increase in social concern and a rapprochement with the working classes on the part of the Church, there was also content whose main objective was to maintain dogmas and traditional practices, in a process of controlling the transformations that had taken place, including in Catholic liturgical rituals.

As the theoretical framework points to the Second Vatican Council as the regulatory framework for the imminent changes, it was decided to catalogue the titles that dealt directly with the Council in a third subcategory. Thus, the three subcategories into which the texts on "reform" were divided were: "updating", "maintenance" and "Council".

In the first year of circulation of O Arquidiocesano, 45 titles were coded that showed aspects of the changes that the Catholic Church was undergoing.

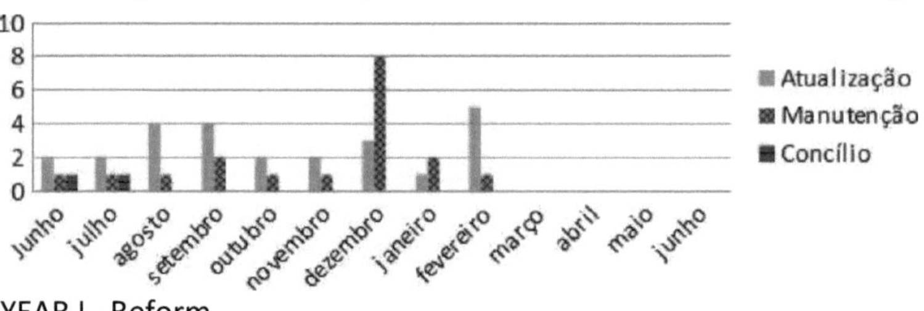

YEAR I - Reform

Twenty-five titles were coded in the "update" category between August 1959 and June 1960. The main subjects covered were the Catholic Action movement, with texts generally signed by Fr Ildeu Pinto Coelho. Eighteen texts were catalogued under this theme in the first year, which corresponds to 40% of the texts in the "reform" category.

In the "maintenance" subcategory, eighteen titles were registered that aimed to direct or contain aspects of the changes in Catholic positioning. Of particular note in this year of circulation was the section Religious Instruction, signed by Fr Belchior Comélio da Silva. This section is generally responsible for the doctrinal nature of regulating practices and maintaining traditional Catholic dogmas. Also noteworthy during this period was the incidence of texts on the indissolubility of marriage and/or against divorce, in defence of the family.

The texts accounted for that year concerning the Ecumenical Council took place in August 1959 and March 1960. The first article appeared in the second edition of the newspaper, dated 16 August 1959. Published in the "Religious Instruction" section, the article is called "The Next Ecumenical Council" and makes projections about the event. The second article, which appeared in issue 28, of 27 March 1960, is a headline on page 3, which states that "The Council Will Attend First to the Problems of the Church".

The second year of circulation of O Arquidiocesano contributed 103 titles to this category. What stands out in this edition is the similar incidence rates between the two subcategories. While there were fifty units of "updating" records, the "maintenance" rates corresponded to forty-nine units. The texts referring to the Council were limited to four units.

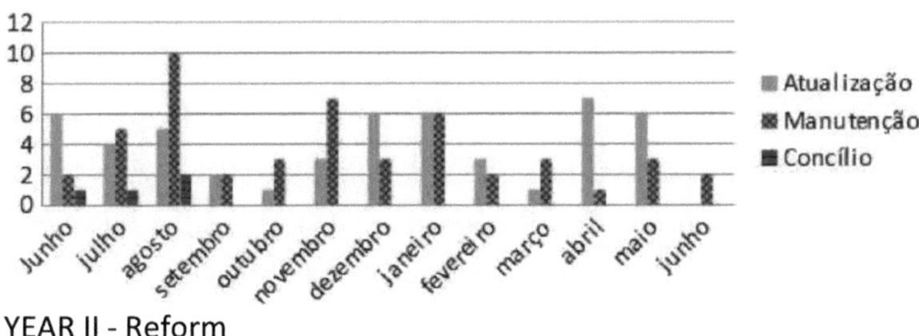

YEAR II - Reform

In addition to Catholic Action, this year the participation of lay organisations in the Church's social works is highlighted. Aspects of the "Social Doctrine of the

Church" are also addressed. Among the texts in the "maintenance" subcategory, the defence of morals, the family, religious education and, once again, the indissolubility of marriage stand out.

Unlike the previous year, in the third year of the newspaper's circulation there was a discrepancy between the incidence rates of the subcategories, with a greater number of texts referring to "updating". A total of 139 recording units were coded, of which 86 corresponded to doctrinal update content. Twenty-four titles were assigned to the "maintenance" subcategory. Also noteworthy in this period was an increase in indexes referring to the Ecumenical Council, with the incidence of nineteen registration units.

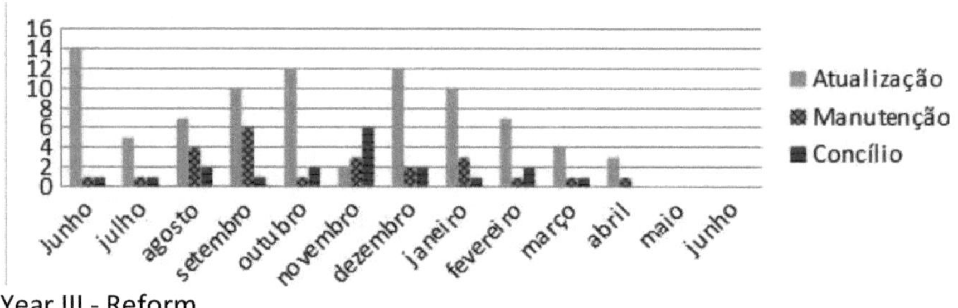

Year III - Reform

Among the updating units, the launch of the encyclical *"Mater et Magistra"* stands out, reflecting an updating of Catholic Social Doctrine. The front-page headline of issue 98, dated 30 July 1961, entitled "Mother and Teacher: John XXIII's fifth encyclical" stands out, in which there is an explanation of the encyclical, as can be seen in the third paragraph, which states that "four great problems challenge modern man and must be resolved in terms of truth, justice and love": "the low level of agriculture in a world whose industrialisation and technology are increasing considerably"; "the enormous differences between undeveloped peoples and technically advanced nations"; "the increase in population, and the imbalance with economic development" and, finally, "the lack of mutual trust that reigns between nations". There is also intense concern about Brazil's agricultural issues. Also noteworthy, between issues 96 and 100, is the repercussion given to the "Meeting of the Bishops of the Rio Doce Basin", at which issues in favour of social development in the region were discussed.

Among the "maintenance" texts are those that defend the traditional family, oppose divorce and promote religious education. In short, the texts that address the Council have a summoning character for the event.

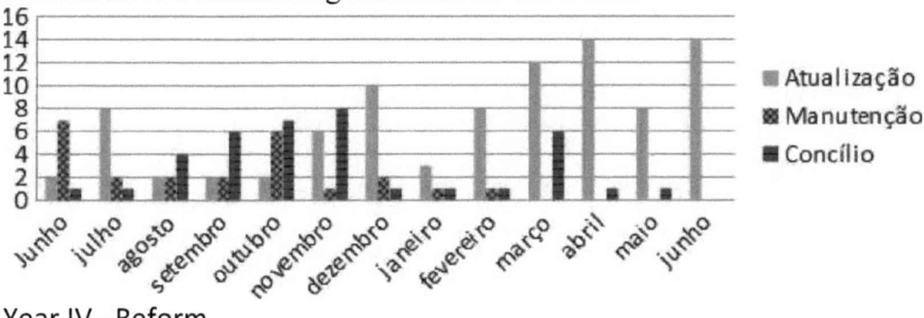

Year IV - Reform

The fourth year of circulation of O Arquidiocesano follows the trend of publishing content that updates Catholic thought. Of the 153 titles catalogued, ninety-one fell into the "updating" subcategory. This corresponds to 59 per cent of the category's registration units for the year. This year, texts referring to the development of life in the countryside stand out, as well as recording units that encourage an advance in Catholic thinking in relation to bringing the Catholic Church closer to other religions. Also noteworthy that year is the 9 June 1963 edition announcing the death of Pope John XXIII.

Another highlight of the cataloguing of data in the year in question is the unprecedented incidence of record units on the Council, higher than the incidence of "maintenance" texts. While the "Council" sub-category was filled with thirty-eight record units, the "maintenance" category had only twenty-four titles. Once again, titles referring to the protection of the family and the defence of morals were predominant among these.

In the newspaper's fifth year of circulation, the subcategories "updating" and "maintenance" became more congruent. While the former registered 87 titles, the latter came close, reaching 79 units. Also noteworthy is the disparity between the two subcategories in relation to the third. While together they account for 90 per cent of the category's registration units, the subcategory "Council" has eighteen titles.

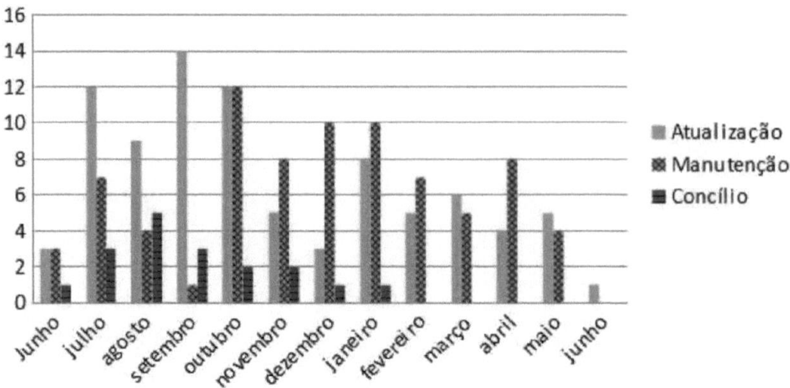

Year V - Reform

Of particular note that year were the first publications issued by the newly elected Pope Paul VI, which already indicated the prerogatives of his mandate. The predominant message was one of continuation and updating of the actions of the dead Pope John XXIII. This can already be seen in issue 198, of 30 June 1963, with the article "The fundamental attitude of Catholics: To love", signed by "MONS. MONTINI, Archbishop of Milan, today Pope Paul VI".

There were also two series of headlines that year, signed by Mgr Oscar de Oliveira, which indicated aspects of the changes that had taken place in Catholic doctrine. The first appeared in editions 204 and 206, of 11 and 25 August 1963 respectively, entitled "Judeo-Christian Fraternity". The second is called "Parish Renewal" and is published between the sixth and twentieth of October 1963, corresponding to issues 212, 213 and 214.

The messages in the "maintenance" subcategory are made up of publications defending morality, the family and anti-divorcists. Of particular note is the endnote on the fourth page of issue 210, dated 22 September 1963, which defends the maintenance of the hierarchy and authority in force: ""There are dialogues that do not destroy the principle of authority and hierarchy; just as there are dialogues that bring about a levelling that is harmful to the Church. Let's keep the former; let's avoid the latter". From November 1963 onwards, the texts that fall into the "maintenance" category appear at higher rates than the doctrinal updating rates.

The sixth year of circulation of O Arquidiocesano began on 29 June 1964, and once again there was a predominance of texts referring to the updating of Catholic thinking on social issues. Of the 234 coded registration units, 135 fell into the "updating" subcategory.

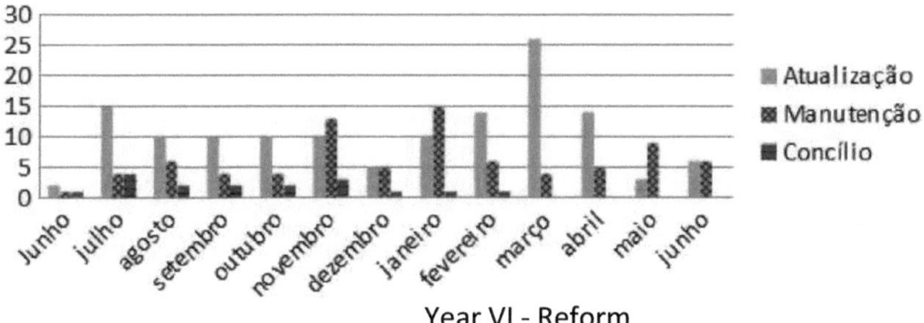

Year VI - Reform

During the rest of 1964, there was a high incidence of texts whose main sign was the word "charity". Between February and April 1965, there were more texts on the CNBB's "Fraternity Campaign". In March 1965 alone, seventeen record units were coded on this theme, a rate higher than that found for the whole subcategory in any of the other months analysed that year.

The highest number of coded texts related to the subcategory "maintenance" was in January 1965. In that month, issue 278, dated 10 January 1965, stands out, with six headlines defending the family. The subcategory also includes themes in defence of the "Catholic faith", "morals" and a series entitled "100 questions about oriental rites", totalling eighty-two registration units. There were also seventeen textual structures about the Second Vatican Ecumenical Council.

In the seventh year of circulation of the newspaper O Arquidiocesano, the incidence rates referring to the subcategory "updating" were supreme. Of all the 237 recording units referring to "reform", 138 follow semantic structures of updating Catholic thought, which corresponds to 58% of the material catalogued for the category. For the subcategory "maintenance", fifty titles were registered, while forty-nine registration units refer to the "Council".

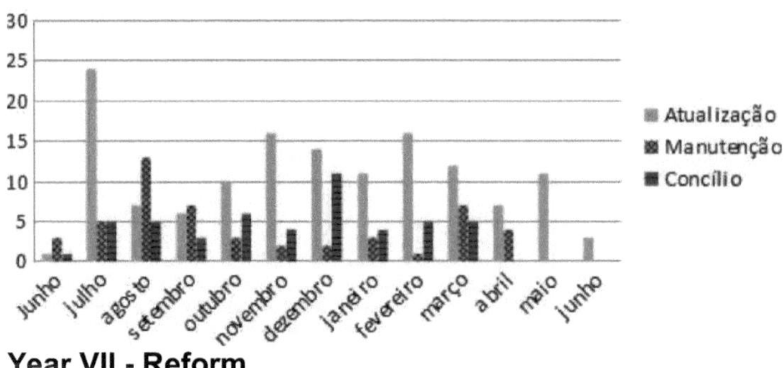

Year VII - Reform

In July 1965 alone, twenty-four registration units were recorded in the "updating" subcategory. The main themes of these texts are the Fraternity Campaign, Catholic Action and the "Lay Apostolate".

The other two subcategories had similar incidence rates. The texts related to "maintenance", reaffirmed the need for "obedience", mentioned the role of fathers in the family and reiterated the discourses against abortion, divorce and in defence of celibacy. The incidence of the third subcategory is concentrated above all in the first half of 1966. Of particular note in this context is the article published on the front page of issue 311, on the twenty-ninth of August 1965, which reaffirms that the "Council does not relax principles: it reinforces them".

The last year of circulation of O Arquidiocesano contributed 179 record units to this category. Of these units, 130 correspond to the "updating" subcategory. Again, the other two subcategories had similar incidence rates. While thirty-one titles were assigned to "maintenance", the subcategory "Council" received twenty-eight registration units.

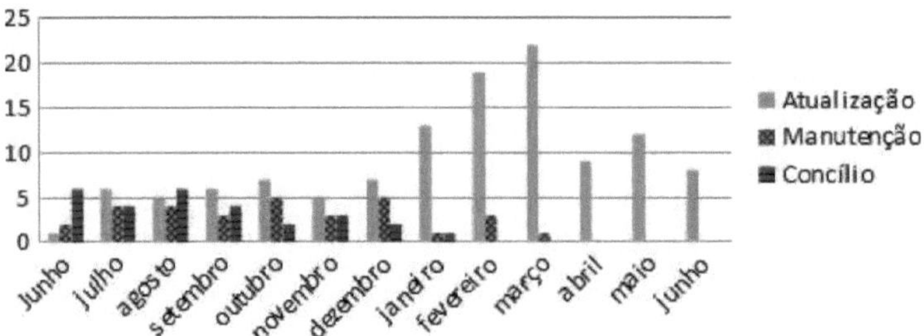

Year VIII - Reform

During 1966, the circulation rates of the three subcategories remained similar. From December onwards, however, the predominance of texts in the "updating" subcategory was consolidated, above all due to the cataloguing of texts referring to the Fraternity Campaign. In March 1967, for example, twenty-two update texts were coded, while no record units were catalogued in the "maintenance" subcategory. This subcategory also saw the incidence of texts, generally arranged in boxes next to the title, advocating greater participation by the "lay apostolate".

With regard to the texts related to the subcategory "maintenance", the predominant themes refer to the indissolubility of marriage and the defence of morality, as in the article in issue 402, of 28 May 1967, entitled "Mini-skirt condemned by Vatican newspaper".

CHAPTER 3

Data analysis: Interpretation

The interpretation of the data collected, which consists of the third part of this content analysis, was based on indices constructed under the sieve of quantitative and qualitative aspects about the "conditions of production" of the messages published by the newspaper O Arquidiocesano. According to Laurence Bardin (2012, p. 45), the process of reaching inferences represents the paths that condition the interpretation of coded data.

> "If *description* (the enumeration of the text's characteristics, summarised after processing) is the first necessary stage and *interpretation* (the meaning given to these characteristics) is the last, inference is the intermediate procedure that allows the explicit and controlled passage from one to the other."

Among the quantitative aspects, the incidence rates of the texts in each category sought to reveal the frequency with which the newspaper O Arquidiocesano published the themes perceived during the pre-analysis phase of the material. These texts were coded to identify their incidence over the course of the months, highlighting some characteristic elements of the approach. Thus, as Bardin (2012, p. 47) suggests, the aim was to analyse the "surface of the texts", or which semantic structures allowed them to fit into the established categories.

The qualitative aspects of the analysis sought to highlight the *"factors that determined these characteristics,* deduced logically" (BARDIN, 2012, p. 47). Thus, the troubled socio-political context of the newspaper's foundation, combined with the frequency with which the texts were published, allowed logical deductions to be made about the relationship between the semantic aspects of the texts and the "inferred variables" of the context in which these messages were produced.

According to Bardin (2012, p. 47), "the analyst's reading of the content of communications is not, or is not only, a 'literal' reading, but rather the highlighting of a meaning that appears in the background". The coexistence of these aspects in the analytical process makes it possible to identify trends and patterns in the incidence of the texts of according to the period in which the messages were broadcast.

> "Or, in other words, what is sought to be established when an analysis is carried out, consciously or not, is a correspondence between the semantic or linguistic structures and the psychological or sociological structures (for example: behaviours, ideologies and attitudes) of the statements."

In this way, the inferences drawn from this work contributed to an analysis of the origin of the statements made by O Arquidiocesano, including its role as the official organ of the Archdiocese of Mariana. In this way, we sought to identify the communication situation constituted in the plot that developed from the publication of the categorised texts.

Among the general inferences observed is the recognition by the Archdiocese of São Paulo of the Catholic Church's participation in the culmination of the 1964 civil-military coup, as mentioned in the first chapter of this work. In this way, the information published by a body that is part of the Catholic hierarchy infer the character of verisimilitude to the corresponding coded data. A specific inference that achieves the same objectives is the interview given by Canon José Geraldo Vidigal de Carvalho in May 2013.

Given the indices generated, related to the context units identified, it became possible to draw up discursive patterns that also made it possible to identify (or deduce) behavioural trends in the universe surrounding the vehicle's affirmation in the social structure of the time.

The first stage of this phase sought to interpret the incidence of texts related to politics that illustrated the participation of the newspaper, and therefore of the Archdiocese, in the ideological climate prior to the civil-military coup of 1964. The supremacy of texts referring to communism reveals the Catholic Church's concern about a possible threat to the social order, which, it should be emphasised, the institution used to maintain its hegemony. By April 1964, 509 texts on this subject had been registered. What's more, the levels of incidence over the years reflect the evolution of Catholic participation in different contexts within the same time frame.

When analysing the newspaper's first year of circulation, we noticed the paper's tendency to direct Catholic thinking against organisations or ideologies that could threaten the reach of Catholic doctrine. To this end, it was noted that all the texts coded in this category referred to opinions against either Freemasonry or communism.

Although concerns about communism were already identified in the first editions of the newspaper, it can be said that the "index of concern", based on the incidence rates, is still minimal compared to the rates in the following years. This can be seen by generating the incidence graph using the years as the units of analysis.

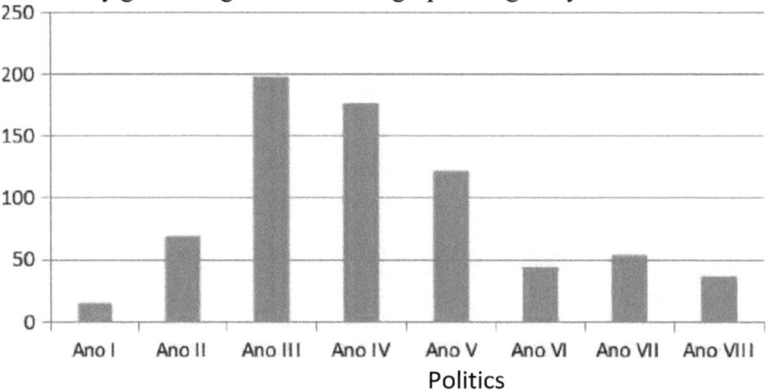

Subsequent years, especially the third year of circulation, indicate an increase in the paper's preoccupation with political issues. This year also stands out because all the texts were coded under the subcategory "communism". The coded texts reflect the relevance given by the paper, especially with regard to issues arising from that year. As well as directly criticising communism, the texts reported on issues relating to land reform and the elections scheduled for October 1962. In both cases, the "communist threat" to private property and "democracy" is a determining factor in the publication of these texts. In addition, during this period there was a need to increase the scope of the content on communism. This can be seen in the series of cartoons entitled "Behind the Iron Curtain". By making the content easier to read, engaging with humour and divided into pictures, it was possible for the content to have a greater reach than just verbal statements in general.

The frequency of texts in the "politics" category during year IV reveals the most obvious behavioural pattern of this content analysis. The similar variations in incidence suggest the influence of the medium on the publications. In the first case, there was a concentration of headlines about the elections between July and October 1962. If we delve even deeper, we can see that most of the doctrinal texts on the 1962 elections were published up until 7 October, election Sunday.

The second variation found refers to the Catholic Church's role in the 1964 military coup. Up until the military takeover of the executive branch, the incidence rates of titles meaning "politics" followed an upward trend. However, after the coup, there was a drastic decrease in the number of texts in this category.

In both cases, the frequency of texts correlated to the respective historical contexts allows us to make deductions about the positioning of Catholic institutions in these events. In both situations, it is believed that once the objectives set for each event have been achieved, the Church redirects its discourse to new needs. Immediately after the elections, the number of texts on the subject ceased. Another article on the subject was only published in March 1963.

Likewise, it is possible to draw conclusions about the paper's positions in the context of the 1964 civil-military coup. The high incidence rates seen until April 1964 plummeted from May onwards. During the first years of the military regime, the incidence of texts on "politics" dropped. It can be deduced that, in this case, Brazilian Catholic thought attributed military intervention to bringing peace and order to the country. Anti-communist propaganda, therefore, tended to be aired less often.

What stands out in the post-coup period, which concerns the editions catalogued from May 1964 onwards, are the changes in the discursive lines of the statements published. The discourse immediately after the military intervention sought to reaffirm that the communist threat still existed and that new articulations were being made by the communists. Despite the reduction in incidence rates, the texts present symbolise a sign of caution, even after the military success.

However, the article "*Empty* stomachs, sources of revolts" is shown once again. In this article, despite the use of figures of speech (such as euphemisms), the military government is warned about its possible unpopularity.

It can therefore be seen that the Catholic Church tries to direct the thinking of the faithful to still fear communism, even after the victory of the "Revolution". However, the most fruitful thing that can be gleaned from this coded data is the induction of possible trends that formed after this period. The reduction in the frequency of texts, combined with this sample questioning the actions of the military government, builds a consolidated inference for analysing other sections of the same research universe. It suggests, *a priori*, that the Catholic thinking disseminated by O Arquidiocesano in the rest of the 1960s tended to move in the opposite direction to that followed by the military government in the same period.

The second category of analysis arose from the need to understand the internal changes that the Catholic Church was going through, before understanding how it positioned itself externally in the Brazilian political context. To do this, we sought to identify which trends the texts related to the adaptations of Catholic indoctrination followed. The theoretical framework indicated the Second Vatican Ecumenical Council as an event convened by the Vatican, responsible for regulating the transformations in the dioceses. Thus, each subcategory had a specific function.

The first subcategory aimed to catalogue all the texts that indicated a change in Catholic dogma or determinations, which symbolised modernisation of rites and/or customs. Contrary to this, the second subcategory aimed to measure the conservative character that remained in the vehicle, or that deserved to be reinforced, in order to avoid trivialising structural reforms. Related to both, the third subcategory aimed exclusively to catalogue texts that explicitly cited the Council, due to its symbolism as a regulatory framework for change.

At first glance, the predominant tendency in this category was to publish texts that update dogma. While the subcategory "updating" included 742 titles, 357 record units were allocated to "maintenance". The subcategory "Council" had 175 texts.

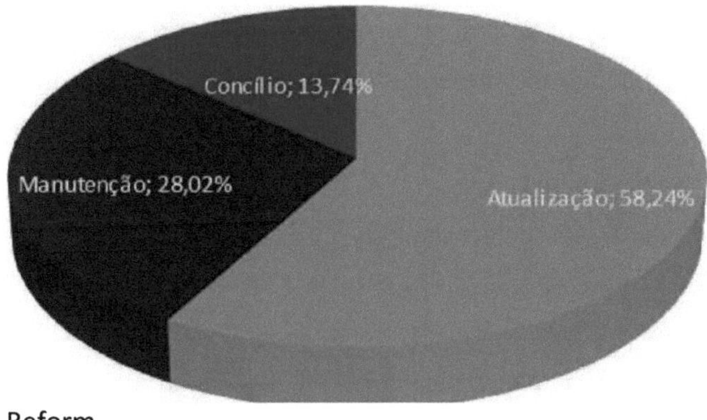

Reform

Although the supremacy of the data coded as "update" can generally be seen, analysing the incidence over the years reveals peculiarities that need to be taken into account. In certain contexts, the rates rise, generating possible interpretations.

The first two years of the newspaper's circulation indicate close levels of incidence between the first two subcategories, which suggests a balance between modernising and conservative actions. Publications about the Council were negligible during this period. Only two registration units were coded in the first year and four units in the second year of circulation.

The following two years saw an absolute majority of texts on being updated. The launch of the "Social Encyclical of John XXIII" stands out. The *Mater et Magistra* Encyclical is a precursor to the Ecumenical Council and establishes the Vatican's guidelines on "the social question". The incidence of content referring to the encyclical contributes to the supremacy of the category in the year in question and therefore makes it possible to perceive the need to disseminate it by the Vatican.

The proximity of the Ecumenical Council and the increase in the publication of statements influenced by the encyclical's social approach contributed to the similar incidence rates. In the third year, there were twenty-four texts on "maintenance" and nineteen on the Council; the situation was reversed in the following year, when thirty-eight units were submitted on the Ecumenical Council and twenty-four on "maintenance".

The specific variables for the fifth year of circulation of O Arquidiocesano reveal inductions about the frequency of texts in the first two subcategories in relation to the atmosphere in Brazil. Although the incidence rates are close, they appear in different contexts in the same year. The supremacy of the "update" texts, seen in the previous two years, continued until October 1963.

From November onwards, the incidence of the "maintenance" category was higher in every month. Based on this data, it can be surmised that the socio-political tension experienced in the country is inversely proportional to the Church's discourse of updating. It is possible, then, that the ideological climate in the country influenced a more conservative and cautious Catholic stance, specifically during this period.

The following years saw a return to supremacy in the number of texts in the updating subcategory. In July 1964, the category regained the highest incidence rate, which would continue throughout the rest of the analytical *corpus*. From the sixth year of the newspaper's life onwards, there was a rise in the number of texts referring to the "Fraternity Campaign". These texts, together with the messages about the lay apostolate and Catholic Action, are the most common units found in this subcategory.

The indices for these years help to identify recurring characteristics of Catholic indoctrination in the period. As seen in the first phase of the analysis, it is possible that the medium influenced the scheduling of news in the newspaper O Arquidiocesano. The messages accompanied the process of updating doctrine up until November 1963. The indices of the two subcategories were aligned during the period of greatest turbulence in Brazilian society, and soon after the institution's "victorious" outcome in 1964, the trend towards adaptation was interrupted.

CHAPTER 4

Conclusion

The coding of 2,402 recording units led to the creation of indices which, in turn, guided the development of this analysis, enabling it to identify trends in the behavioural pattern adopted by the Archdiocese of Mariana and disseminated (explicitly or not) through its official communication vehicle.

We can see that the context in which the newspaper was founded has its own peculiarities and, far from it, can be analysed as a homogenous structure. As such, the environment in which the newspaper is inserted is fundamental to the perception of aspects that induce the Church to act on the issues analysed.

In order to understand the evolution of Catholic thought in the concepts that guided this analysis, it was necessary to break down the text/context relationship into various semantic time sections. In the end, these sections could be related and, in turn, make it possible to identify the trends and intentions of the vehicle and, consequently, of the institution.

In general, the political statements made by the newspaper reveal a tendency for the Catholic Church to be concerned about the social turmoil in the country. While the "politics" indices show a high incidence of texts opposing communist ideology, the reform indices reveal a tendency for the institution to take a stand on social issues. In this way, it is believed that the Brazilian Catholic Church in this period was looking for ways to fill the gaps in its area of influence, areas that could be occupied by other emerging organisations. It can therefore be seen that the purpose of the decisions taken by the institution in this period was to guarantee the permanence of the social structures in force.

One behavioural pattern observed refers to the use of The Archdiocesan as a campaign platform for disseminating content that directly impacts Brazilian society. The incidence rates increase with each need that arises. This occurs, for example, in the subcategory "elections" in 1962.

The texts are concentrated in the months leading up to the elections. On a larger scale , there were a greater number of texts referring to "communism" in the years of greatest turbulence in Brazil.

The codified materials related to the civil-military coup contribute to a broader analysis of the relationship between the Catholic Church and the Brazilian state. Attached to the theoretical framework, they make it possible to see that the Catholic institution allied itself with the state in Brazil's three anti-democratic experiences: Brazil Empire, New State (Getúlio Vargas) and Military Dictatorship. However, in relation to the military period, the indices reveal a change in Catholic thinking, related to the military government's loss of popularity.

The "reform" category is developed, above all, in the process of evolution of Catholic thought, tending towards discursive lines determined by humanitarian and social statements. However, the incidence of texts in the "maintenance" subcategory reveals the institution's need to control transformations that directly affected the area of application of Catholic doctrine. This could be illustrated by the content used in maintenance discourses. Several texts are concerned with Agrarian Reform (many in defence of private property and/or concerned about the rural exodus); with the indissolubility of marriage (in defence of the traditional family) and in the "defence of morals".

It is believed that these trends allow logical deductions to be made about the use of O Arquidiocesano as a thermometer of the ideological climate surrounding the troubled period when the paper first appeared. However, cataloguing this data makes it possible to carry out in-depth analyses based on smaller or more specific (semantic or temporal) sections. This work merely reiterates the fertile field for linguistic, discourse, media, identity and representation analyses that arises from reading the pages of O Arquidiocesano.

To this end, we have endeavoured to make the data coded in this analysis available as a way of highlighting scientific initiatives in this area, the history of the Mariana press and the relationship between the media and power. The indexes can be consulted at goo.gl/6R3QvN .

CHAPTER 5

Bibliographical references

ARCHIDIOCESE OF SAO PAULO. **Brazil: never again.** São Paulo: Vozes, 1985.

AZZI, Riolando. **The Catholic Church in Brazil from 1950 to 1975.** Chronological list of facts, episodes and relevant statements.

BAHIA, Benedito Juarez, 1930-1998. História, jornal e ética: história da imprensa brasileira, volume I - 5 ed. - Rio de Janeiro: Mauad X, 2009.

BARDIN, Lawrence. Content Analysis / Lawrence Bardin: translation Luís Antero Reto, Augusto Pinheiro - São Paulo: Edições 70, 2011. Reprint of the 2011 edition.

FERREIRA, Jorge and DELGADO, Lucília de Almeida Neves eds. **Republican Brazil. The time of the dictatorship - Military regime and social movements at the end of the 20th century.** Book 4.

Rio de Janeiro: Brazilian Civilisation, 2003.

BOTAS, Paulo Cezar Loureiro. **The blessing of April: "Brazil, urgent": memory and Catholic engagement in Brazil, 1963-1964.** Petrópolis: Vozes, 1983.

BURKE, Peter; BRIGGS, Asa; **A Social History of the Media: From Gutenberg to the Internet.** Translation by Maria Carmelita Pádua Dias. 2.ed. rev. and arnpl. Rio de Janeiro: Zahar, 2006.

CAMACHO, Ildefonso. **The social doctrine of the Church: a** historical approach. Edições Loyola, São Paulo, 1995.

CASTRO, Marcos de. **64: conflito Igreja x Estado.** Petrópolis: Vozes, 1984

DUSSEL, Enrique. **History of the Latin American Church (1930 to 1985).** Paulus, São Paulo. 1989.

ELIAS, Norbert. **On Time.** Rio de Janeiro: Zahar, 1998.

FICO, Carlos. **Beyond the Coup: the seizure of power on 31 March 1964.** Rio de Janeiro: Record, 2004.

HABERMAS, Jiirgen. **Structural change in the public sphere.** An enquiry into a category of bourgeois society. Rio de Janeiro: Tempo Brasileiro, 2003.

LAGO, Cláudia; BENETTI, Márcia (eds). **Research methodology in journalism.**

Petrópolis: Vozes, 2008. 2ª ed.

MELLO, José Marques de. **História Social da Imprensa.** Porto Alegre: EDIPUCRS, 2003.

MOTTA, Luiz G. **A construção da narrativa do tempo presente.** *Contracampo,* 12, Iº sem./2005, p. 23-49.

PENA, Felipe. **Theory of journalism.** São Paulo: Contexto, 2008. 2ª ed. 3ª reprint.

REUTER, Yves. **Analysing narrative.** São Paulo: Difel, 2002.

RICHARDS, Pablo. **Morte das cristandades e nascimento da Igreja;** translated by Neroaldo Pontes de Azevedo; revised by Luiz Antônio Miranda; São Paulo: Ed. Paulinas, 1982.

TRAQUINA, Nelson. **Theories of Journalism II: The journalistic tribe - a transnational interpretive community.** Florianópolis: Insular, 2. ed., 2008.

CHAPTER 6

ANNEXES

Annex 1: The image of the rosary allied to a bullet and "0 canto do soldado brasileiro" are from 5 April 1964. Four days after the outbreak of the civil-military coup.

Mariana, 19 de Abril de 1964

O "Arquidiocesano"

Nova Lepanto, Incruenta, Salva o Continente Americano

Brasil, de Rosário na mão, derrotou a invasão comunista

Liturgia da

Annex 2: The civil-military coup is presented as a bloodless victory against the communist threat on 19 April 1964.

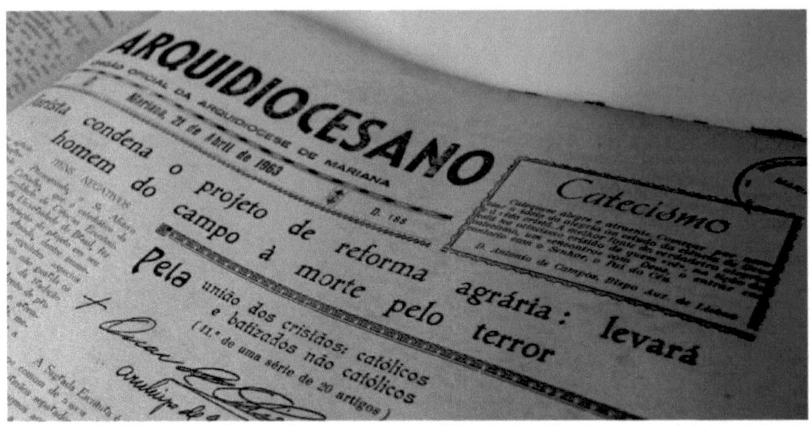

ARQUIDIOCESANO

Órgão Oficial da Arquidiocese de Mariana

Mariana, 21 de Abril de 1963

Catecismo

... condena o projeto de reforma agrária: levará homem do campo à morte pelo terror

Pela união dos cristãos: católicos e batizados não católicos

(11.º de uma série de 20 artigos)

Annex 3: The agrarian reform proposed by João Goulart is criticised in April 1963.

...riana, 19 de Abril de 1964

...da Propagação da Fé

Comunismo, automatismo, inimigos da alma

Cleveland, U. S. A (NC) — O homem de ciência não pode alcançar o progresso de sua disciplina ao preço da fé religiosa, advertiu aqui ... John J. Wright, bispo de Pittsburgh ... o prelado ao Grêmio Alberto Magno ... de homens de ciência.

Sem a fé não resta outra alternativa ... comunismo ou automatismo.

... mito do poder ... máquina como simples ...

Annex 4: Communists are seen as enemies of the soul.

Annex 5: Cartoons against communism began to appear in 1961.

2 Mariana, 24 de Maio de 1964

"O Arquidiocesano"

Contra o comunismo e a desonestidade

Imprensa Católica

Annex 6: The "revolution" of 1964 was to wipe out the communists and the dishonest.

Mariana, 9 de Dezembro de

Histórico da Infiltração Comunista em CUBA

Annex 7: The newspaper criminalises communist experiments in other countries, December 1962.

Printed by Books on Demand GmbH, Norderstedt / Germany